A BEGINNER'S GUIDE TO
GLASS ENGRAVING

Seymour Isenberg

Published by

**krause
publications**

700 East State St., Iola, WI 54990-0001
715-445-2214
www.krause.com

Please, call or write us for our free catalog of antiques and collectibles publications.
To place an order or receive our free catalog, call (800) 258-0929. For editorial comment and
further information, use our regular business telephone at (715) 445-2214

Library of Congress Catalog Number: 00-101579
ISBN: 0-87341-900-6

Printed in the United States of America

Front and back cover pieces by Jan Matuszak, Sutdio One Art Glass, Milwaukee, Wisconsin

Other Books from Krause Publications

How to Work in Stained Glass, Third Edition,
by Anita & Seymour Isenberg

Glass: An Artist's Medium,
by Lucartha Kohler

Introduction to Lapidary,
by Pansy D. Kraus

Enamels, Enameling, Enamelists,
by Glenice Lesley Matthews

Silversmithing,
by Rupert Finegold and William Seitz

Modeling in Wax for Jewelry and Sculpture, Second Edition,
by Lawrence Kallenberg

For Kim Kostuch of Studio One in Milwaukee, Wisconsin, Holly of the Denver Glass Company of Denver, Colorado, and Calvin Sloan of the Star Bevel Studio of Riverview, Florida, for their help in the production of this book. What is useful herein is due to them; any errors or misstatements are the author's. And to my wonderful partner, Patricia Daley, who lessens the confusion.

Contents

Introduction

Why a book about glass engraving as a hobby? That question can, of course, be asked about any craft and especially one not as yet necessarily in the mainstream of popular conception. Many years back the same question came up about stained glass when I was looking for a publisher for my book How to Work in Stained Glass. The question was "Who would be interested?" This question was answered a year or so back by the third edition of this book being published over a period of 25 years, and a whole new audience developed for this now well-accepted hobby.

Not that glass engraving is an adjunct to stained glass; not at all. While glass engraving can be incorporated into the stained glass armamentarium, as will be seen in the course of these pages, it is basically a stand-alone modality. No stained glass knowledge is necessary to provide yourself with lovely fabrications developed through this technique; however if you are already working in stained glass, glass engraving can be a wonderful inclusion to the work you are already doing. If you have never worked in stained glass or had any glass experience, don't let that stop you. What techniques that are applicable to glass as a whole will be introduced at the proper place, will be explained, and their relationship to glass engraving will be made clear.

For glass engraving is fun; that's probably why you've become interested in it. A hobby should be fun. Mostly it is a one-to-one relationship, as is any handcraft: it's your imagination working through the medium of glass to project something of yourself that will fill you with the pride of accomplishment. Few things are more satisfying to hear than the question, "Did you really make that?" It's something you'll hear a lot once you start in this field.

But there are other advantages to glass engraving besides boosting your ego. It's work you can take up and put down at will. If you don't have time to complete a project at the moment, it will wait for you tomorrow or the next day. It won't go bad. There's no stress, no strain. If you make a mistake or change your mind after doing some lines you don't like, you can throw the glass away and start again. Even if you are working on a beveled piece, the glass is expendable.

And you can take your time. The work will wait for you to return to it even if it's a month or more. You can engrave for hours, or you can spend a relaxing ten minutes. There's no paint that has to be fired, no solder that will oxidize, no mess to clean up (well practically none). Nor do you need a lot of space to indulge this hobby; it can be done in a corner of an apartment room as readily as a basement or a studio setup, though remember, you do need an electrical outlet and a source of water.

It's important to emphasize that what is discussed in this book is specifically stone wheel engraving. Copper wheel engraving, while similar in many instances, is a much more intense and more difficult subject to master. You can get finer lines and more of a graphic flow with a copper wheel than with a stone wheel, but more patience is required and more technique. It's also a much slower process. However, when you learn stone wheel engraving and should you desire to expand to copper wheel engraving, you will find that you already have staked out a lot of the territory

I mentioned bevels. In many instances the glass that you will be engraving will be beveled pieces. This is not incontrovertible. You can certainly engrave on any glass surface and not necessarily plate glass, but a bevel seems, with its slanted edges, pretty much a perfect canvas for engraving to many engravers. Beveled glass may be purchased as such, usually machine made from a "line" beveler, or you may want to have the fun of making your own bevels to your own specifications. For this purpose I have included a chapter on how to make bevels and, hopefully, how to enjoy making them. Thus the entire process of engraving, from making your bevels to imposing upon them the designs of your choice, may be found within these pages. The end result is, as one master engraver has put it, "a work of the spirit."

At the same time, this is a book for beginners and as such I concentrate not on complicated advanced projects but on practice pieces using the various wheels and hand motions. Stone wheel engraving is a matter of "hand sense," a combination of timing and motion and pressure. The pressure comes from the manner of holding the glass against the turning wheel, not (as some might think) the wheel against the glass. Engraving, as I use the word, is done on the lower glass surface as you hold it against the wheel and look through the glass from above. The various wheels make varied impressions and learning how to use these wheels and the machine that employs them is the basic purpose of these chapters and will take up most of the book. Once you understand how pressure and motion produce the various shapes, putting these shapes into an aesthetic progression will be up to you. With the information provided here, you should be able to start, as well as advance to more complicated work.

Si Isenberg

Chapter One: Beginnings

Some General Remarks at the Start

There are several ways of imposing a permanent design onto a glass surface: sandblasting, acid etching, painting, or merely scratching with a carbide tipped "pen" will provide, depending on the user's skill and goals, a final result that can be lasting and, to the extent that it is skillful, effective. Some might add that just cutting the glass with a glass cutter imposes a design of sorts, though this is more a practical than an aesthetic end result.

The effects of different shaped engraving wheels. Row 1: the olive wheel, Row 2: the printy wheel, Rows 3 and 4: the mitre wheel, Row 5: (left) the mitre wheel demonstrating drag, a technique of moving the glass to opaque a portion of it.

An attempt to engrave glass using a dremel tool (basically a hand drill) holding a grinding stone or wheel. This very unsatisfactory result demonstrates why I use an engraving machine.

Of all the above methods, the art of stone wheel glass engraving is perhaps the most spectacular and, if I may use the term, the most free-wheeling. Not only does the engraver end up with a prismatic array of sparkling depths and translucencies, he has at his disposal the means to control the precise nature of the cuts without the additional burden of first providing a resist material as is necessary in sandblasting and acid etching, or incurring the additional risks of kiln firing, which must be done when painting. The stone wheel glass engraver enjoys a stand-alone situation that is lacking in all other impositions onto that provocative surface.

The sheer delight of being able to place your design as an immediate accomplishment provides a great sense of satisfaction. And, despite a certain amount of popular opinion to the contrary, wheel engraving is not an esoteric, exacting art, requiring years of training and expensive equipment. Of all the glass working endeavors, wheel engraving is prob-

ably the most compact and user friendly. Of course, the more exacting you become and the more you practice, the more jewel-like and impressive the end results will be.

Mastering the proper techniques at the start will add facility and efficiency to any craft; acquiring the equipment necessary to do wheel engraving is no more outrageous or expensive than any other phase of glass art. A lot depends on individual goals; the more you want to advance in a craft, the more exacting you become, the more equipment you amass.

A Brief Glossary

Bevel: a glass shape, usually plate glass of varying thicknesses, the edges of which have been angled by machine to allow light to be broken up into prismatic colorations.

Bushing: the process of filling the center hole of an engraving wheel with lead when a tapered mandril is to be used.

Casting table: a small table with a circular top of steel into which concentric circles have been cut. It is specific for bushing engraving wheels that will be used with a tapered spindle (mandril).

Chipping: see Roughing

Circle cutter: a device to "cut" circles in glass. There are a number of such items from small to large. The larger ones hold the cutter to the glass by means of a suction cup.

Dalles de verre (also known as "slab glass"): These are 1" thick glass squares of varying colors. Usually they are not susceptible to engraving unless they are clear.

Dremel tool: A hand tool that will accept various bits for grinding, polishing, or drilling.

Dressing: a term applied to engraving wheels that are being shaped into one of the three basic profiles.

Dressing stick: this silicon carbide stick is used for dressing engraving wheels. Hand pressure on a wheel turning on the engraving machine allows the wheel to be "dressed" to whatever shape the operator desires.

Elbow protectors: any soft material that prevents your elbows from resting on the hard surface of the worktable.

Engraving: as used in this book, a method of using stone wheels to impart a design into a glass surface.

Engraving machine: a lathe-like device with a motor, a dial to control revolutions per minute, and a shaft that runs steady and true; in effect a precisely machined apparatus to engrave glass.

Flashed glass: glass that has one color placed over another so that when the engraving wheel removes the top color, the bottom one shows through. Such glass is frequently used for "aciding" or etching.

Foiling: the act of wrapping a piece of glass with premeasured sticky-back copper foil to enable it to be soldered to a neighboring piece.

Glass cutter: a specific device to score glass. Glass is never "cut" since it is in essence a liquid. It can be scored, however, that is a fracture line can be imparted upon it with a device called a glass cutter.

Grozzing: the act of chipping away pieces of glass using a specific type of instrument called grozzing pliers.

Hand piece: similar to what a dentist will use; used in crafts similarly to a dremel tool.

Mandril: see Spindle

Mandril key: a device to unlock the mandril from the shaft. A flat screwdriver may also be used for this purpose.

Mitre wheel: a stone wheel with a surface ground to a point.

Olive wheel: a stone wheel with a surface rounded to produce an olive-like impression on glass.

Printy wheel: a stone wheel with a curved surface that will make a circle on glass.

Roughing (chipping): making the sides of a center hole of a wheel irregular so as to hold a bushing more securely.

Running pliers: a pliers designed to "break out" a score line in a piece of glass.

Score line: the groove imparted to a piece of glass by the wheel of a glass cutter.

Soldering: the use of a hot iron to melt solder onto copper foil or lead to hold pieces of glass together (in this instance).

Spindle (also called a mandril): the device that fits into the shaft of an engraving machine to form the axle (shaft plus spindle equals axle.). In engraving, spindles or mandrils can be either tapered (coming to a point) or straight (blunt). In both cases, the end of the spindle has been machined with spiral grooves to hold an engraving wheel.

Strap wheel: a stone wheel with a flat surface pretty much as it comes from the manufacturer.

Craft Applications

For the hobbyist/craftsperson who has armed himself with the basic techniques of stained glass, adding the process of wheel engraving is like opening new horizons. But you don't need to have worked in any other glass field to grasp and enjoy this sparkling technique strictly on its own.

Stone wheel engraving is an end in itself with no dependency on any other glass techniques. However, it may be combined with other glass disciplines. Beveling (the technique of angling the edges of plate glass for a prismatic effect) or stained glass (cutting and placing into a pattern glass that has been colored in molten state by the addition of metallic

A glass engraved stand-alone bevel lit from behind shows some of the delicate tracery involved in its design.

oxides) are two possible auxiliary disciplines. However, working in the field of glass engraving alone will allow you to turn out an almost unending line of delicately wrought creations once you learn to use the wheels. These may have a life as individual items or be incorporated as centerpieces in single or dimensional windows, or as etched sections of a flashed (two-colored) stained glass work; or as a design in a single plate glass bevel, or even imparted into clear dalles de verre, (6" squares of glass 1" or so thick). In short, engraved glass can remain as singular artifacts or be amalgamated within other creations, adding luster and sophistication to varied projects.

Types of Glass

Plate glass. Glass for engraving is mostly of the plate variety, that is glass that is considerably thicker than the single strength window glass most people are familiar with when they think of glass as such. Such thickness allows the engraver to cut deeply into it and certain designs might require such deep cutting, which gives a sort of bevel within the glass that can break light up like a prism. Clear plate glass can

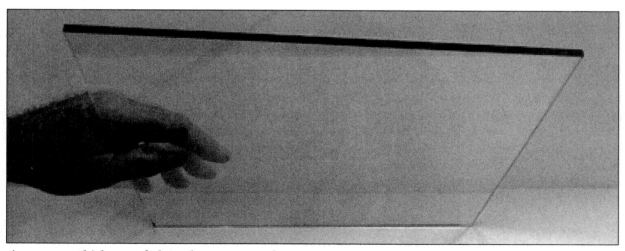

An average thickness of plate glass seen on edge.

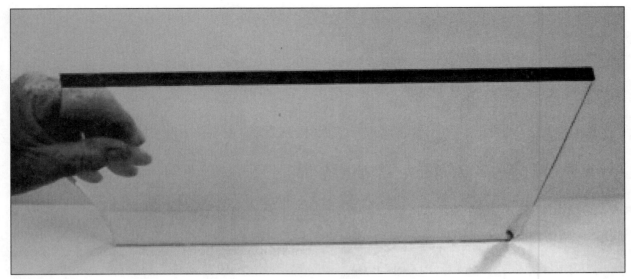

A really thick piece of plate glass seen on edge.

vary enormously in width. Be careful here. In choosing a piece of plate glass to engrave, you don't want to work with one so heavy that it's awkward to hold. Also watch out for scratches, since most engravers use plate glass scrap they acquire from a local glass shop. Somehow the scratches never seem to show up until the engraving is just about done, when they appear to ruin the work to a greater or lesser extent.

Double strength glass. As it implies, a glass not as heavy as plate but thicker than the standard single strength. You can engrave on such glass and the impositions will look good, but, obviously, you can't go very deep here.

Antique glass. Mostly a term used in the stained glass industry. This glass is colored in its molten state by the addition of iron oxides and is mouth blown in the factory. It tends to be irregular in thickness and is rarely used for engraving purposes.

Cathedral glass. Machine made colored glass, either opalescent or clear.

Opalescent glass. Opaque glass of one or many colors.

Flashed glass. As described previously, a glass that has one color "flashed" or placed atop another. Such glass, if the bottom color is clear, will provide a spectacular effect when used for engraving.

Equipment

You will need several essential items. The equipment pictured will serve the needs of the advanced worker as well as the beginning hobbyist. Detailed photos and descriptions of all these components appear in subsequent chapters.

The Process

The engraving process consists of two distinct parts: pre-engraving, which involves preparation for the actual glass work, and engraving, which is the application of the principles and products of the pre-engraving considerations.

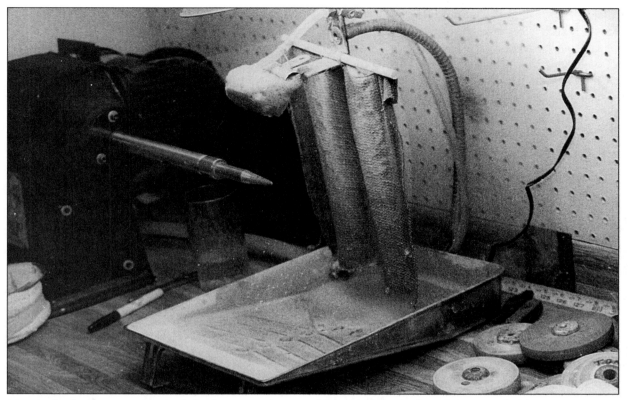

Here's the basic setup. To the left, the engraving machine with its shaft and the mandril (or spindle) protruding over the drip pan, which catches the water from the waterline above, which wets the sponge, which lubricates the wheel. The little curtain hanging behind and below the sponge protects the back wall from being splashed by water. The wheels that fit on the mandril are shown to the right of the drip pan.

The pre-engraving process includes checking that the engraving machine is running true, balancing the engraving wheels (bushing), using the casting table, a special device to ensure a proper wheel balancing, preparing the mandril (that portion of the engraving machine that holds the wheel) for proportionate sizing of the wheel, and insuring a proper water supply.

There are also other aspects of the pre-engraving routine that will be gone into in a later chapter. I think the main thing to keep in mind here, and it is something that many beginners fail to understand, is that one cannot just walk up to an engraving machine and start engraving glass. There is a good deal of preparation involved, much of it individualized to the job in hand, but a lot of it general. You should be prepared in your initial encounter with the subject, to find the subject, at first, somewhat elusive.

When I talk of wheel engraving throughout this book, I am discussing stone wheel engraving. The basic process involves holding the glass against a turning stone wheel (not the other way round, which is how some people visualize the scene) and moving the glass in such a manner as to regulate the depth, length, and flow of the cuts to create a design. Sounds simple, right? Such a design can vary from a couple of crossed lines to an extremely complex geometric pattern or motif. Part of the fun of the craft is that even crossed lines by themselves can be pretty spectacular.

To repeat, stone wheel engraving involves two steps: the pre-engraving (preparation) portion and only after this, the actual glass working. The pre-engraving portion is as critical as the more dramatic glass impositions and a lot of time must be spent on it if you want your work to turn out properly.

There is another type of wheel engraving. This other type uses a diamond or carborundum or copper disk and, while many of the techniques overlap and the basic premise is pretty much the same, the process is essentially more expensive, more difficult, more intense, and is not addressed in this book.

Stone glass engraving and wood lathe carving have a certain common ground. In both instances a design is imposed on a yielding surface; in both cases the movements of the artist's hands and arms control the end result. Also in both cases, not much formal training is required; the machine does the heavy labor. The point is that you don't have to be an "artist." No art background is necessary, though the end result may give the impression that you have such. In fact, glass engraving, like stained glass in general, is so spectacular that even flawed work tends to look good, at least to the untrained eye. Any-

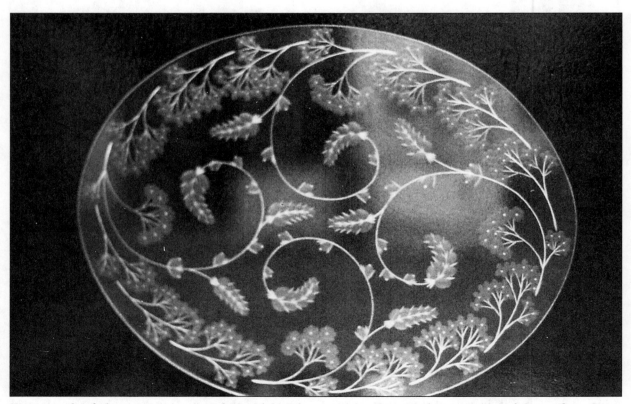

An example of glass engraving on a large plate. The engraving covers a large portion of the surface. Courtesy of Studio One, Milwaukee, Wisconsin.

one can engrave, provided they take the trouble to learn how to use the engraving machine and the various stone wheels properly, and spend time practicing their arm and hand movements that are so necessary to a satisfactory end result.

The heart of the wheel engraving process is the wheel. There are a number of wheels and each must be balanced and shaped by the worker before any piece of glass can be engraved. The initial chapters of the book address just these processes. Beginners tend to find this necessary grooming of the wheels somewhat tedious since they have their hearts set on starting to engrave glass immediately. Unfortunately, without a series of proper wheels, there is no way you'll be able to turn that desire into reality. It's best to realize at the outset that a certain amount of preliminary work is necessary before you even touch a piece of glass. And if you have any sort of tool sense, you'll come to enjoy creating the correctly shaped wheels and prize them for the intricate devices they are as well as for what they will enable you to accomplish.

Intaglio Vs. Relief

Glass engraving is really a form of intaglio. Intaglio is the process of carving a design beneath the surface of the selected material, which looks as though it is within the surface. In glass engraving, the design is cut into the bottom side of a piece of glass but gives the effect of standing out from the surface nevertheless. The opposite of this technique is called "relief" engraving where the design really does stand out from the surface, having been truly cut away from it. In relief engraving, the background must be ground away to leave the jutting foreground. Such a technique is not glass-friendly (to put it mildly) and is outside the purpose of this book.

In this book, you will be involved with intaglio - from fairly simple to some rather complex designs using (mostly) plate glass as a medium. A specific design, once you have turned out a couple of dozen of them and your hands have sensed the requisite motions, may then be carried in your head, but any new work should have a design drawn directly onto the glass. Get in the habit of doing this as a beginner and you will find that following a design will become second nature. There are workers who have been engraving for years who can improvise designs onto glass just by having them described, but you're not quite that good yet. For now, place your design ideas directly on the glass surface (see page 121).

A Few Perceptions

As in any modality, there are always individuals who insist on hearing their own music no matter what the band is playing. Many are full of misguided potential but are too impatient or too idiosyncratic to take direction. A word of warning at the start: Don't start any craft, much less glass engraving, unless you are prepared to follow instructions and take advice. Nothing can turn you off engraving faster than a badly balanced wheel turning to no avail, burned glass that ends up making a mockery of all your efforts, shaky movements that St. Vitus himself might disown, insufficient light, or any of the other factors that will swarm faster than mosquitoes once you start "winging it."

Glass engraving is a hobby that can easily become a profession, but there's no law that says you can't keep it within your boundary lines should you wish to do so. As in any craft, the more you work at it, the more adept you will become and the more artful and complex will be your end results. Keep in mind that engraving is a skill as well as an art. Anyone is capable of learning the skill. No book, including this one, can teach the art. That comes from within the craftsperson, but the first step toward art is learning the skills. Development of such skills is what you will find herein.

A word of caution. An engraving machine is a long term investment. If you can possibly use someone else's to begin with, that is the least expensive way to begin. If you find you are using someone else's machine to the point where you want to steal it, it's time to get your own.

Chapter Two:
The Work Area

There are three absolute necessities for the glass engraving work area and slighting any one of them will handicap your efforts to turn out professional looking engraving work. First of all, your work area should be properly lit. It is astonishing to me how many beginners try to work in inadequate light. Second, you must have a convenient source of water. And last but not least, you need a stable workbench.

The work area in a major studio. All that's needed to turn out beautiful looking engraved designs is a table area, good lighting, and an engraving machine. A water supply may be incorporated with a small hose from a nearby sink but some source of water must be available. Courtesy of Studio One.

Lighting

Engraving is close work, so you need to see what you are doing as fully and with as little eye strain as possible. The nature of the material you are working with - glass - means that lighting should be arranged to throw as little shadow onto the work as possible while providing back-lighting without glare or unwanted highlights.

While fluorescent lighting can be used as the overall illumination, I have found it helps considerably to have a regular incandescent lamp (a gooseneck works well) throwing over-the-shoulder light directly onto the work. This kind of pinpoint illumination is excellent to spot flaws. Such light can also be used as a "bounce-off" to focus with during the engraving process. Having this kind of light literally on top of the work allows you to regulate the light as you need it. This is more convenient than having to keep turning the work around to get the best illumination from the ceiling and usually getting in your own way. Aside from any other consideration, such a maneuver is uncomfortable and you want to be as comfortable as possible when you are engraving.

Daylight

Daylight is an important part of the general lighting scheme and if you are working in a room that provides such (alas, much glass work is done in basements or garages with little daylight access) you should take advantage of it. After all, holding a piece of engraved glass up to the light usually means holding it up to the sun to get the most effect, so daylight is really the final judge of the completed project. If possible, I like to hold my work up to the light of day even as it is progressing so I obtain a true perspective. Too direct sunlight, however, can give false readings as far as highlights are concerned and you should keep this in mind and perhaps modify this kind of glare by working through a piece of tinted glass. Sunglasses might help here.

The curved hose behind the drip pan brings water to the cutting wheel. Courtesy of Studio One.

Artificial Light

Artificial light should be used against a dark background so you can more easily see what is happening on the glass surface as you progress. Placing your engraved project on a piece of black felt works well to check your progress as you go along. Black cardboard will also work. The most efficient placement is directly in front of you as long as you position the felt or cardboard so it doesn't get wet from the water stream as you work.

Water

Without a constant flow of water over the wheel, you cannot engrave. You don't require a flood here, merely a drip; however even a drip will mount up so you will have to contend with arranging some sort of drainage situation. It isn't necessary for this to be as ornate as some workers arrange, with a circuit of waste water going through a conduit. You can get by easily enough with a simple drip pan that can be easily emptied when required. A metal paint tray works well for this purpose.

One caution: Do not empty your waste water down the drain of your sink. The water will contain a sludge of glass particles from the grinding process plus ground stone material from the wheel itself. This material is not digested well by indoor plumbing. Dispose of the water waste in dirt in your back yard, but please not in the flower bed, where you may work the soil with bare hands. To save trips back and forth, I empty my water tray into a large bucket nearby. As the waste water sits in the bucket, as in the pan, the sludge settles on the bottom. It is tempting to use your fingers to scrape this sludge out. Not a good idea. There may be some small but very sharp bits of glass in there that will remind you of its potency in other areas than the aesthetic. Best to use a scoop of some sort that doesn't bleed.

Regulating the Water Flow

A siphon system is fine to maintain a proper water drip even if you are going to be

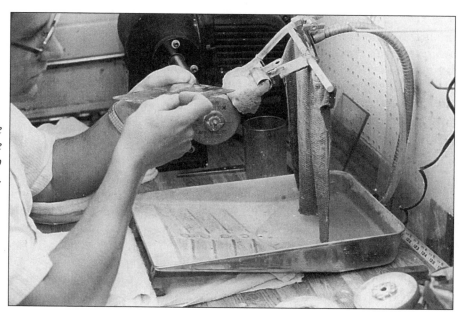

In this work station, the water comes through the curved hose behind the drip pan and into the sponge, which wets the wheel.

doing a lot of engraving. If you want to arrange the drip to come directly off a pipe, that will work even better. That's the method I prefer. A gravity-fed system, however, will do the job. It can be as simple as a plastic jug with a tube coming out the bottom or a 15-gallon bucket hanging from a hook in the ceiling. You can have a gravity-fed system that sits on the table as well, but keep in mind that 15 gallons of water at a pound a pint will add measurably to the weight on that side of the table. Depending on the type of table you are using, that could be a problem. You don't want the table tipping over. On the other hand, such a weight can be used to counterbalance the pressure you create when you lean on the table during the working process.

Gravity-fed systems can easily provide enough water for a lengthy operation without the necessity of replenishing constantly and thereby interrupting the work procedure. One individual I am aware of ingeniously uses an IV bottle with a stand acquired some time ago from a local hospital. However, most intravenous material now comes in plastic throw-away containers. If you can acquire some of these items, including the tubing, you can have a rather unique setup for a continuous drip modified by some sort of clamp to regulate the flow. Alternatively, you can use the tubing from any fish aquarium. The water, whatever the apparatus you arrange to get it to drip, will drip, not directly onto the wheel or the work, but onto a sponge.

The Sponge

The sponge is held by a clasp to a stand and sits directly behind and upon the wheel, the idea being that the water it contains lubricates the stone as it turns against the glass. Obviously, it is critical that the proper amount of water flows onto the sponge. Too much water will create splashing and prevent you from seeing what you are doing. Too little water will allow the wheel to "burn" (overheat and scarify) the glass. If that happens, most likely you will have to start over. You can control the amount of water in the sponge by tightening or loosening the spigot initially. This may sound at first like something of a trial, but it will soon become second nature.

As you go along you will shortly learn by trial and error how to regulate the drip so that just the right amount of water fills the sponge. You must remember, however, to turn the water off when you are taking a break, and turn it back on once you start to work again. A common mistake of beginners is to forget to keep an eye on the water in the excitement of actually engraving the glass. But the water is as much a part of the engraving process as is the glass. Providing the proper flow of water must become second nature if you don't want to ruin the same project over and over.

Elbow Protectors

As the name implies, elbow protectors protect your elbows, which act as the support elements of the triangular posture you assume while working. Your elbows will bear the brunt of your weight against the workbench hour after hour. Don't attempt to do glass engraving without some form of elbow protection, not for any length of time. The ulna nerve (called the funny bone) travels in a groove in the elbow and constant pressure on it will cause numbness of the fingers. This will improve neither your disposition nor your work.

You can buy protective "sleeves" ready-made in surgical supply stores but it is much cheaper to make elbow protectors yourself.

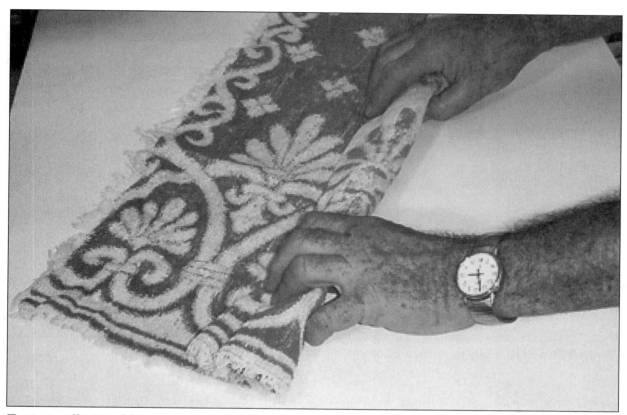

To start, roll a towel into a tight strip. A medium size towel is best.

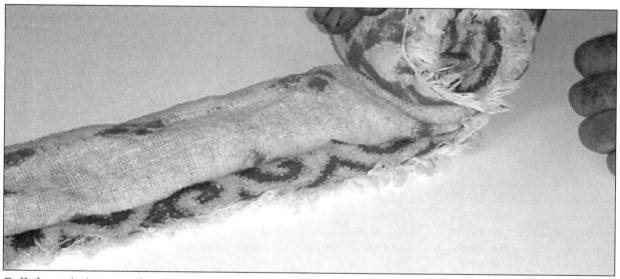

Roll the strip into a coil and tape around the circumference.

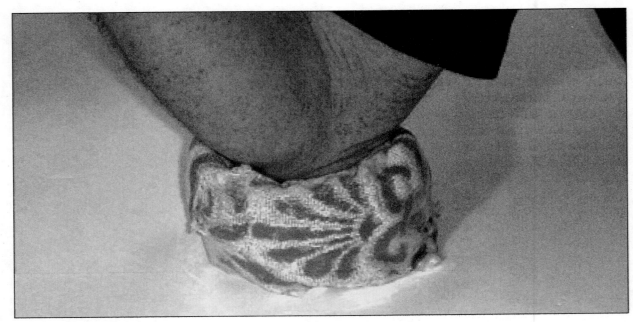

Your elbow will be nicely cushioned while you work.

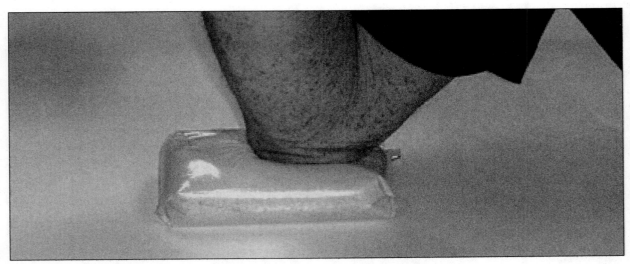

Fill a heavy duty freezer bag with sand for another type of elbow protector.

Without elbow protectors you will start to get pains in your fingers from leaning against an unprotected surface. This one is made by folding a towel into a long strip, rolling up the strip, and wrapping it with tape to form a coil. When it gets dirty, just take off the tape and put it in the wash.

The best elbow protectors I have found are made with rolled up towels held with tape in a coil and placed upright on the table. When the towels get dirty, just put them in the laundry and reroll them. Unlike sand pads they don't slide on the table but allow for the motion of the arm as transmitted to the elbow, and they are easy to get used to.

Some workers use sand pads which can be as simple as an old sock or plastic bag filled with sand that they place on the table-top for the elbows to rest upon. I tried this and find these still irritate the joints after a while and that my elbows tend to slip over the plastic. Towels, to my mind, are best.

The Workbench

Since you will sit in front of this workbench for long periods of time, you want to build in some comfort as well as strength and efficiency. Your workbench should have the height and conformation for you to be at maximum ease as you work. If you are left-handed, you should arrange everything to compensate for this. Engraving, unlike stained glass work, is almost always done sitting. You are entitled to sit comfortably even if you only intend to be engraving for a short period of time.

The posture you assume in your chair should be reflected in the design of your bench. When you sit, you should have both feet flat on the floor, not dangling. Your bench should allow your thighs to be relaxed. By no means should you be cramped or impinged upon by the surface of the workbench.

Standing does occur, however, when you dress the wheel. "Dressing" the wheel means getting it back as close as possible to its ideal cutting shape following extensive use. This requires procedures discussed in Chapter Five. For the moment, allow that the leverage standing provides makes dressing the wheel easier, but for most engraving you will be sitting. You may want to stand if you are engraving an exceptionally large piece of glass, since this might be awkward to accom-

The proper stance for engraving. Note that the elbows bear the weight of the operation and are protected from the hard tabletop by coiled towels. In this position, the work is exactly the right height and completely under control, and the operator is comfortable with good sight lines. This position can be held for a long time without fatigue. Courtesy of Studio One.

plish while sitting. At least 90% of the time, however, you will be sitting, fortunately, since sitting for eight hours (the usual workday in large studios) is far more comfortable than standing for that length of time, unless you are sitting awkwardly.

Position is Everything

Usually the glass pieces you engrave will be small and won't cause a weight problem, so you can calculate your workbench height to maintain your hands at shoulder level as you lean with your elbows on the workbench top. Your upper and lower arms will form a triangle to provide the proper comfort and the proper strength to engrave. This triangle will provide the requisite force to anyone doing the work, whether you are young or elderly, whether a weight lifter or fashion model. This triangle is where all your force comes from. Maintain it, calculate for it, utilize it, and you will never have to worry about the engraving machine

going its own way. You will be in control. However, if you are careless and don't abide by this triangle, you will end up fighting the machine all the way and have little joy in the process.

Needless to say, your bench should be sturdy, free from any sort of movement, and well anchored to the floor. Theoretically a concrete bench would meet these specifications but since this is impractical, compromise by choosing or building a good solid wooden bench, nothing rickety, nothing that will give under the weight of the engraving machine or the water carrier or from you as you exert the requisite pressure on your end of the bench.

The Space

You don't need a lot of room to engrave and there is very little mess from material being thrown about, as can be the case with beveling (see Chapter Eight). Beveling is closely allied to stone wheel engraving, but is basically concerned with angling the edges of thick plate glass so that prisms are formed. The grit and cerium oxide used on the wheels that are necessary for beveling tend to fly about and make a bit of a mess if one doesn't take steps to avoid it.

You will pretty much stick to water and the engraving stone wheel as the sole components of the engraving process presently under discussion. Rarely, if at all, will you employ grit and cerium oxide, the one for excessively coarse engraving and the other for polishing. And, since the water is regulated to a drip, you can do your engraving in a reasonably compact space. So be reasonable in this regard. I don't recommend using your kitchen or living room. A portion of a basement or garage will serve even if it doesn't have a window for outdoor light, though it is nice if some daylight can be accessed.

You don't need a lot of air circulating either, since the water keeps the glass dust down. For the same reason you don't need to wear a special mask. In fact, glass engraving probably takes up less room and is more accommodating to an existing space than any other work with glass. It is practically a self-contained procedure. However, that doesn't mean there are no safety requirements, the main one being to protect the eyes. Always, when engraving, wear safety glasses.

Slat Racks

Glass that is left lying on the table prior to use in either the beveling or the engraving process is subject to various evil possibilities. Usually such pieces tend to pile up and this can lead to slipping around the table, sticking together, and scratching or nicking of the surfaces. Mostly it leads to wasting time as you search for the piece you require at the moment. If you are working with more than

one piece of glass at a time, either in beveling or engraving, it might be well worth your while to build a slat rack.

A slat rack is a simple wooden frame with slats cut into it and thus designed to keep the glass pieces standing up and separate from one another. Slat racks have many advantages. In addition to keeping your glass pieces disparate and thus able to be readily categorized, they allow you to overview any project at a glance and to be able to pick up and put down each piece you are working on easily and comfortably.

Thus, at the beginning of any multiple piece project, cut out all the glass pieces and stand them in the rack. Then rough each piece and put it back in the rack. I do this routine through all the stages of the engraving or beveling procedures so that at any moment I can glance at my slat rack and know exactly where I am. It's a lot easier than having to constantly be looking for the next piece of glass scrambled with others on the table and possibly in worse shape than when I put it down.

Such slat racks are extremely useful in large studios where many jobs are being done at one time. Here the racks prevent confusing the pieces of one job with another, especially where people are working in tight quarters. But even if you are only working on a single job with only a few pieces, you will find a slat rack most useful.

Safety First

As stated previously, use safety glasses all through the pre-engraving and engraving processes. This isn't because chips of the cutting wheel fly about and might get in your eyes. Such would be extremely unlikely since wheels used for engraving are very strong. Actually, engraving wheels are recommended

Showing rough cut glass ovals on slat racks. These are waiting to go to the first beveling station. Although these glass pieces are shown lying down because they are too thick to go in the slats, as they are beveled they will fit in the slats.

All these pieces will be first beveled, then engraved.

for speeds three times faster than you will ever need for stone wheel engraving. These wheels can run up to 4000 rpms; the normal engraving speed is at 1000 rpms.

While it's a billion to one shot that a chip of wheel will come flying out at the engraver or at anyone observing the engraving process, what may happen is that water may fly away from the wheel toward an unprotected eye. In that water will be suspended glass particles and wheel slough (portions of the stone that are ground away with use and mix with the water). This would not help your eye much and is bad enough, but there is also the possibility of a piece of sponge taking to the air. This is most likely to happen when you first start work, when the sponge may still be dry and friable. Such a missile has all the above spent particles trapped in it and if something like this hits you in the eye, it could mean serious trouble. So no matter how often you have done engraving without mishap, don't become careless. Always wear your safety glasses.

Clothing and loose hair - both can be dangerous. Keep anything likely to catch in the spinning wheel either tied back or at a distance.

Fingernails aren't really a safety feature but the fact is that long nails will very likely become quite short. Nails just get too close to the wheel, especially when you are manipulating small pieces of glass. It's just as well since you can't do detail work with long nails. Even short nails tend to get engraved.

Chapter Three:
The Machine and the Wheels

The Engraving Machine

Since the engraving machine is an exquisitely precise piece of equipment, I don't suggest you attempt to build your own from spare parts you may have lying around the yard. In the long run, unless you are a machinist well aware of the necessities involved and have access to the necessary ingredients, I suggest you purchase your engraving machine

The engraving machine I favor, the EG-1 from the Denver Glass Machinery Co. It comes complete with all the parts and template for mounting to your worktable. It is completely plumbed with a knife edge spray head on the polishing side of the machine and flexible water supply and sponge holder on the engraving side. The stainless steel shaft and spindles are precision machined, providing a smooth true running shaft. The bearings are neoprene mounted to eliminate any vibration. The 115 volt 1/3 horsepower SCR variable speed motor allows the operator total control from 100 rpm to 1200 rpm. Morse taper spindles allow for quick change and perfect centering of wheels. One 5/8" straight threaded spindle is included. Dimensions: 36" long x 24" wide x 19" high.

The left side of the engraving machine has a threaded shaft to which wheels with 3/4" holes can be mounted for polishing an otherwise completed engraving. Polishing, also called "brilliant work" is usually a term applied to very deep cuts which by nature reflect light more than shallow ones; it is also used when polishing any type of engraved or beveled pieces with (usually) cerium oxide or jeweler's rouge.

from one of the companies that make them. One such is the Denver Glass Machinery factory. I've seen jerry-built equipment that some wanna-be engravers try to pass off as engraving machines. They appear to be prouder of their machines than the poor quality engraving such put-together devices produce. You really should decide at the start if your time is best spent trying to build an engraving machine or engraving.

The best way to assure yourself that the machine you purchase has all the prerequisites necessary to engrave properly is to get one from a reputable company that will unquestionably stand behind its product. Again, the Denver Glass Company has been making such machines for a long time and is the company I recommend.

Once you set out to buy a machine, however, there are several features you should look for that are crucial. The studio engraving machine must be versatile within the limits of its purpose. It should be able to comply with any modification in engraving technique - from very fine work on small pieces to more extensive sweeps on large pieces of glass.

Here are some requirements of an engraving machine to allow for maximum versatility. Please keep these in mind, for without these essentials you cannot engrave.

1. Variable speed control. Certain applications require very slow rotation of the wheel. In some cases the wheel may look to be practically at a standstill. Nevertheless, even at such a minimum rotation, it has to maintain the same power it has at a fast speed. This ability of a spinning wheel to maintain the same thrust at practically a standstill as at a fast spin is called "torque" and it is actually a function of the engraving machine, which imparts it to its shaft, which imparts it to the wheel. Such a wheel, even at very slow speeds, will not allow any impedance to change its rpm. The speed range of a wheel should go from zero to a full rpm of 1700. Usually a speed control dial (rheostat) is provided with the ranges of variable speeds that the particular machine will accomplish.

2. An off/on switch. This should be conveniently accessible. The last thing you need is to be fumbling for the switch in the middle of concentrating on your work. The switch should be placed on the machine so that it neither catches on the edge of the table nor interferes with hand motion.

3. Along with torque (see #5), your machine must have an absolutely steady shaft. Turn the machine on and place your hand around the shaft to make sure it doesn't wobble. It's easy to feel if it does. You may not be able to see

small defects at this point (there may be some wobble that you will have to compensate for later), but you should be able to note any gross defects.

Not only should the shaft be steady, but it should also be the proper length. Such length is presumably standard but you should nevertheless check to make sure your hands will have enough room to maneuver the glass you intend to engrave without hitting the body of the machine.

4. Also essential is the correct horsepower motor. As noted before, I prefer a machine that will take the wheel up to a full rpm of 1700. That's probably more speed than you will ever use, but with that kind of excess power backing you up, you can be certain of getting the rpms you need for all operations. The average engraving rpms will be about 60% of what such a machine can provide. I

usually engrave at about 1100 to 1200 rpms but you will have to find out for yourself as you progress, what speed is best for you. My advice would be to start off at fairly slow speeds, maybe 800, until you get the feel of the stone against the glass. The faster your wheel runs, the more control you may lose, especially as a beginner. If you take your time and don't hurry the process, the speed you need will work itself out.

Considerations will vary according to the complexity and size of the work you are doing as well as the type of wheel you are working with. There is no absolute rule of thumb here. In engraving, more than almost any other craft, individuality of technique is the key to turning out good work.

The description "a sturdy motor" does not mean something that will take you to the moon. However, a 1/3 horsepower

Here's a good example of torque. The operator in this picture tries to slow down the turning shaft with his hand, but the harder he grips the shaft, the more force the shaft generates through the torque factor built into the motor. Torque can thus be thought of as a counter force. This is also a good view of the basic engraving setup. Engraving doesn't take up much room. All you need is a good machine, a source of water, a well-placed sponge, a drip pan, a selection of wheels and some elbow protectors. The engraver does not come as part of the supplies.

motor is not adequate. A one horsepower motor, on the other hand, is over-powerful for what you need. You will need at least a 1/2 horsepower motor for normal operations and this is what your engraving machine should provide. If you intend to get into some sort of production situation (many hobbyists do) where you will be doing a lot of engraving day after day, a 1/2 horsepower motor will be quite adequate to carry you through such tasks. This will be the case even if you end up using wheels as large as three feet in diameter.

You may wonder why you would ever use a wheel that large. Probably as a beginner you wouldn't. The fact is, a large wheel covers a wide area and its outer perimeter spins much faster than that of a smaller wheel. It will therefore remove material (glass) much more rapidly than a smaller wheel. Where such rapid removal is required, a small wheel would likely break down, or at the very least, prove unequal to the task. However, such large wheels are not the norm and I mention them here only to allow that they exist.

5. Torque. Torque is as much a function of the motor as is horsepower. Torque applies to the amount of power behind the turning of the shaft. Unlike horsepower, torque is not a measurement of the amount of work the motor can do, but is a measure of function and applied to the wheel that shaft is turning.

Any engraving machine worth the money, if it is to operate properly, must have a constant torque mechanism. That means that whatever speed you select, the same turning force will be maintained no matter what the wheel encounters. This is not something you can readily appreciate when you are purchasing an engraving machine. You can, of course, turn the machine on to slow revolutions and then grasp the turning shaft and try to slow it down. If you can slow it down,

don't buy that machine.

To best appreciate this somewhat confusing quality, think of torque as a counter force to your own strength. When you are engraving, you put a strain on the engraving machine's motor, for you will be pushing, in some cases quite forcefully, against the spinning wheel attached to the shaft being turned by the motor. Depending on the thickness of the cut you want to produce, you may be exerting more pressure in this one instance than you have ever done. Without the torque mechanism, such pressure could slow the motor down. This would be counter-productive for the engraving process. Indeed, it would probably ruin the work quite rapidly. To overcome such a lack of torque you would have to keep varying the speed of the wheel to respond to your pressure. That would lead to madness. What you require is a constant speed. But without torque, the harder you would press on the wheel, the less work you would accomplish, since you would constantly be slowing the wheel. You might even stop the motor altogether.

The constant torque mechanism built into the engraving machine prevents this slowing down due to external pressure. The wheel, because of torque, must maintain a constant turn of the shaft no matter how much pressure you put against it as it turns. A constant torque factor means that the harder you push against the wheel, the more power is generated by the machine to overcome your pressure. So as soon as strain against the motor increases, the motor compensates. It is important to understand this for two reasons. First, without the torque factor you cannot engrave; second, because of it, certain additional safety precautions must be observed.

It is critical to remember that if something gets caught in the turning wheel or shaft (such

The back of the motor of the engraving machine, showing the off/on switch and the rheostat for varying the speed.

as your necktie or a lock of hair), the shaft will not stop turning. In fact, the motor will increase power to overcome the impediment (as it sees it) with possible unfortunate consequences. I've heard of individuals who have had hair pulled right out of their heads due to torque and their own carelessness. That's another reason you want the off/on switch immediately accessible. Memorize its position and make a reach for it instinctively at the first sign of anything getting literally out of hand.

Variable Speed

As mentioned earlier, variable speed is a necessary factor in standard engraving machines. Now that you understand how insufficient torque allows the motor to slow down when you don't want it to, you can imagine occasions when you will want the motor to slow down. Such occasions occur not from pressure against the wheel but specifically by the rpms being

decreased. To allow for this, your machine must be equipped with a variable speed control, that is to say, a rheostat.

Fine engraving can't occur without a means of modifying the speed of the wheel. This means your motor must operate on direct current; so you must have a transformer to convert the alternating current that comes from all standard outlets. Alternating current motors allow no way of internally controlling their speed. They operate at constant rpms that can only be modified by the use of belts. Belt adjustments are inconvenient, tedious, provide erratic speeds due to wear, and waste time for maintenance better spent on engraving.

Before direct current motors were available, the belt system was used for engraving machines. Such machines used a series of pulleys to move different belts, maybe five or six, to produce various speeds. Once the direct current motor came along, it became possible to vary the speed of the motor directly by use of a converter, or transformer, built directly into the motor; a much more satisfactory arrangement and one that allows you a great advantage over engravers of the past.

The Axle (Shaft and Mandril)

The axle is a critical portion of the engraving apparatus. You cannot achieve fine results unless the axle is absolutely true. I cannot stress enough that the axle must be long enough to do the proper job and it must remain absolutely steady during work.

There are two parts to the axle: the shaft, which I have already mentioned and is further described below, is the long steel tube leading from the motor. It is actually part of the motor. The other part of the axle is the mandril (or spindle), which attaches on one

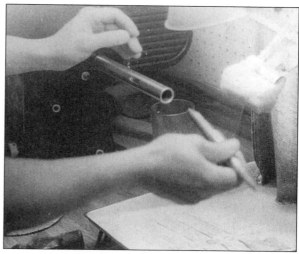

The open end of the shaft ready to accept a tapered mandril (or spindle, the terms are interchangeable).

side to the shaft and holds the engraving wheel on the other side. Both the wheel and

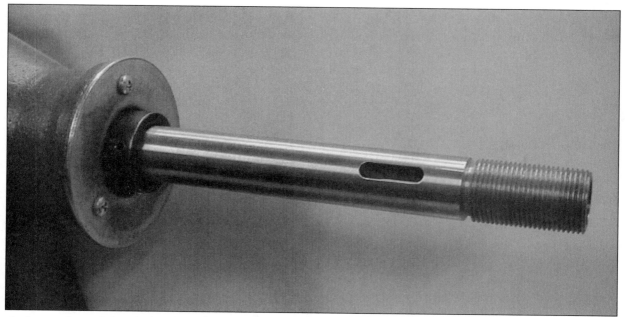

A closer view of the shaft. The 2-3/4" threaded section at the end accommodates a variety of engraving devices, including wheels. The slot in the side is part of the key-in-lock mechanism that holds the spindle in place.

mandril (spindle) should be readily removable so they can be replaced when required during the engraving operation with the least effort. The shaft is not removable.

The Shaft

The shaft is not just an ordinary steel tube. It is specially machined with a #2 Morse taper. This may mean nothing to you, but it is important to know because the measurement is a standard in the industrial lathe industry and the engraving machine is, essentially, a type of lathe. Using a shaft with this standard measurement makes it possible to acquire mandrils (spindles) that will automatically fit such shafts. Remember that the shaft plus the mandril or spindle forms the axle. The mandril is what holds the wheel and permits its use. If you had a shaft measurement made to individual specifications, you would have to special order every size mandril to fit it, as well as every ancillary device pertaining to the shaft. Fortunately, you don't have to do this. If you want to change a mandril for one of a different dimension you can be sure the replacement will fit the shaft. Since there are two types of mandrils, tapered and threaded, and there are different dimensions available of each, you can see how awkward it would be if they were all made to individual specifications. Whether you prefer tapered or threaded mandrils, all are available for this standard size shaft. Interchangeable parts is the name of the game.

Tapered and Straight Mandrils

The mandril or spindle holds the wheel to the shaft. The mandril itself is attached to the shaft by a lock-and-key mechanism that makes it easy to remove and replace. Of the two types of mandrils, tapered and straight (also called threaded, though both are actually threaded). The difference is in the type of end holding the wheel. The tapered mandril is just that, a piece of steel that comes to a threaded point upon which the wheel is screwed; the straight (also called threaded) mandril is blunt rather than pointed and allows for the wheel to be held by a nut screwed over the threaded end.

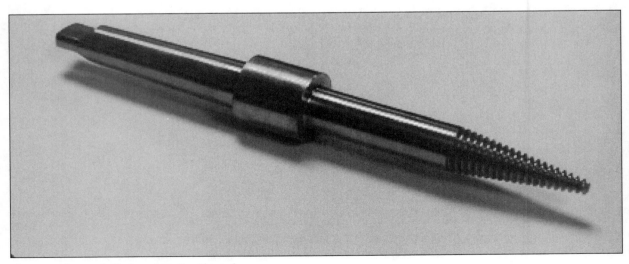

A tapered mandril showing the threads..

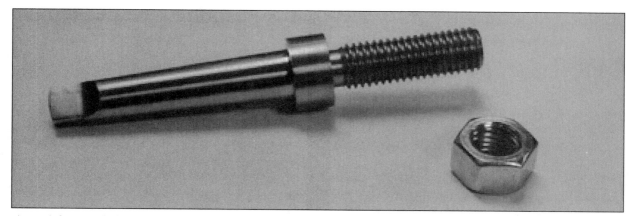

A straight mandril showing the threaded area and the nut that will hold on the wheel after it's threaded on.

Fitting the wheel to the tapered mandril involves more of an initial process than does the straight mandril, to which the wheel is simply threaded on and held by a nut. Though the tapered mandril makes it easier to change from one size wheel to another very quickly, using tapered mandrils requires that the wheels be "bushed" before they can be mounted on the mandril. Bushing means filling the center hole in the wheel as it comes from the factory with a material that is strong enough to take the forces that will be applied, yet maneuverable enough to hold the wheel to the threads of the tapered mandril. The bushing material must also be flexible enough to allow the wheel to unthread when it is necessary to be changed and a new one applied. While the bushing process does take some extra time initially, I prefer it over using straight mandrils because it lets me change wheels more readily and (I feel) holds the wheel more firmly during the engraving process.

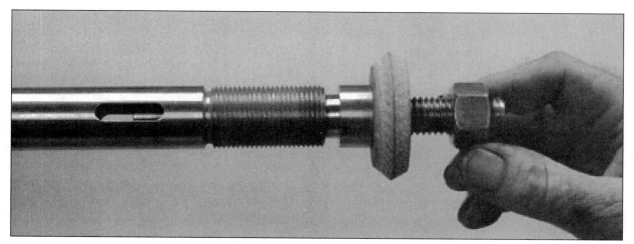

Locking a nonbushed wheel onto a straight mandril.

A straight threaded mandril coming out the end of the shaft. Note the left side of the mandril collar where it butts against the shaft. The rest of the mandril is inside the shaft and cannot be seen. The right side of the collar may have a washer placed against it to help support the wheel when it's in place and act as a rough leveling guide. The thread of the mandril goes right up to this collar, allowing the nut to be tightened snugly against the wheel.

If you don't want to go through the bushing procedure you might prefer straight mandrils. All wheels come from the factory with a standard 5/8" pre-molded hole in the center. You can order any size wheel and it will still have this size center hole.

Compare the straight mandril in the photo to the tapered mandril. The threaded portion of the straight mandril is meant to fit right through the center hole in the wheel and the wheel then butts against the unthreaded "collar" or shelf of the mandril where the threads

Tightening the nut to hold the wheel in place on a straight mandril. Don't over-tighten this nut or you might break the wheel. Simple hand tightening will suffice.

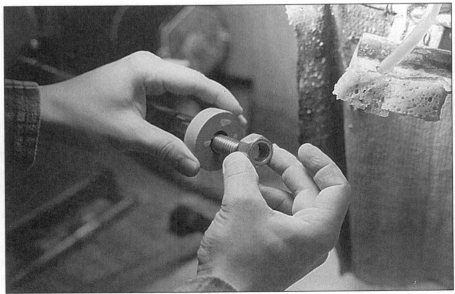

A straight mandril with a wheel and nut attached.

A tapered mandril with a fully-bushed wheel attached.

end. Once the threaded portion is through the hole, a nut is applied and the wheel thus made secure. It's a simple operation and eliminates the extra work of bushing the wheel that is necessary with a tapered mandril.

Unfortunately, not all center wheel holes are absolutely precise since they are mass-pro-duced and not held to strict calibration. In addi-tion, every engraving machine's axle may have slight idiosyncrasies of its own, no matter how strictly machined. Once you put on the nut to hold the wheel in place, you may find there is a slight shift of the wheel up or down when it is turning. This can be most annoying. The shift doesn't have to be much to keep you busy mak-ing constant adjustments to get the wheel pre-cisely balanced. While such adjustments will also be necessary with a tapered mandril, once you make them you shouldn't have to keep making them every time you change wheels because the bushing will see to it that each wheel goes on the same way each time. With the straight mandril you will likely find you have to make minute adjustments every time you change wheels. After a while what you start grinding are your teeth.

Holding the Mandril to the Shaft

The mandril is held to the shaft with a wedge-type lock. Thus it can be put into the shaft very firmly and rapidly and removed

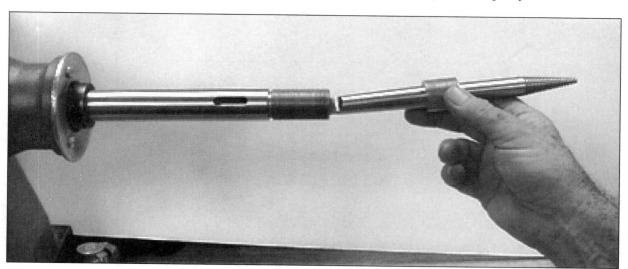

Placing a tapered mandril into the shaft.

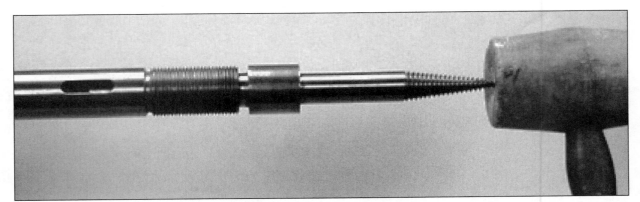

With the mandril in the shaft and locked in with hand pressure, the end is tapped, not too hard, with a hammer to make sure it's seated completely.

The tapered mandril locked into the shaft

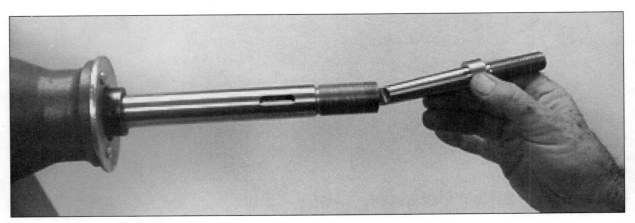

Placing a straight mandril into the shaft.

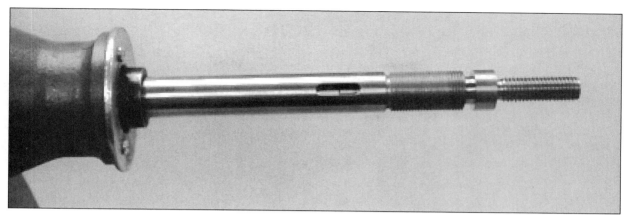

The straight mandril locked into the shaft.

equally rapidly. In, out. It literally wedges in, and once it's in, it's a very secure and tight fit.

Remember that the shaft and the mandril are two separate pieces. Students frequently ask why this is. Well, suppose the mandril becomes damaged, as is certainly possible considering the stresses imposed on it. If the axle (mandril and shaft) were one piece, you

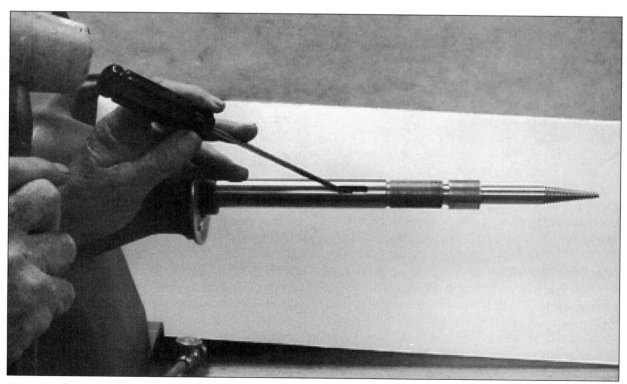

You can also use a flat-blade screwdriver to release the mandril from the shaft.

Getting the mandril out of the shaft is what that slot in the body of the shaft is for. A special key that comes with the engraving machine can be fitted in this slot and the end is tapped with the hammer. This forces the mandril out of the shaft. Once you tap the key, it is self-supporting and the final tap allows you to remove the now loosened mandril.

would have to remove the shaft from the machine and have it relathed. You would have to search for a special shop to do this, and even if you found such a shop, it would be expensive and probably result in an unsatisfactory device. With the mandril essentially a separate working entity, if anything untoward happens to it, you can either straighten it yourself (there are special bending irons for this) or substitute another mandril. It makes more sense economically as well as practically to change just the mandril rather than to change the shaft as well each time you want to change a wheel. That's why the mandril and shaft are two pieces forming the axle, with the mandril able to pop in and out of the shaft.

The holding device that imposes the mandril upon the shaft, thus producing the axle, is a key-in-lock with a 180° variation. You simply push the mandril into the shaft and give it a tap with a hammer - a tap, not a blow. Once it's in, it's impossible to remove by hand. One little hammer tap thus makes the shaft and mandril a (temporarily) permanent axle. Caution: Before inserting the mandril into the shaft,

make sure it's clean. Any grit or surface foreign matter will interfere with the precise fit necessary to hold these two pieces together.

When you want to change wheels, you can remove the wedged mandril with a wedge-shaped key that comes with the engraving machine. This key fits in the slot in the shaft and when tapped (not slammed) with the hammer, the mandril comes loose instantly.

Wheels

The engraving wheel is what actually marks the glass and thus imparts your design, so obviously you want to acquire the best for the purpose. The "best" is a qualitative term - engraving wheels are made, not born. A number of qualities may be looked for when purchasing wheels: how true in shape; how balanced; whether the center hole is truly in the center; what material it's made of; its size and so forth.

Most wheels coming straight from the factory are various standard sizes from 30" x 3" x 2" to 1" x 1/4" x 5/8" and, important to note,

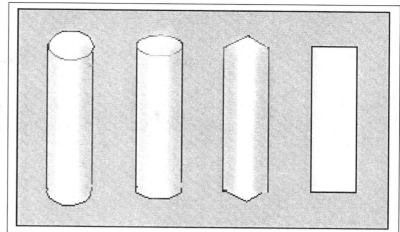

Four shapes of engraving wheels, left to right: printy wheel, olive wheel, mitre wheel, and strap wheel.

are not shaped for engraving purposes. Shaping the wheel (dressing) is a process discussed in Chapter Five. For the most part, wheels come with a flat edge, though there are some exceptions to this (diamond wheels). A "V" wheel and a "printy" wheel (a wheel formed to produce a specific shape on glass) are available as diamond wheels from the Denver Glass Machinery Co. No matter what size wheel you start with, as you work with it, it will get smaller, so you may not want to buy very small wheels to begin with.

Wheels for use with the engraving machine I prefer (the Glass Engraver EG-1) may be made from various materials since the EG-1 is capable of doing crystal cutting and stone or copper wheel engraving on any size piece of glass. Almost any type of wheel can be used, depending on what you have in mind. Wheels for polishing can be made of cork or felt impregnated with a polishing compound like cerium oxide or plain; those for actual engraving can be cast-iron or steel or stone or diamond wheels. Diamond wheels work the fastest (too fast for my taste) and are, of course, the most expensive. Cast-iron and steel wheels can only be used in the shape in which they come from the factory and therefore their

use in engraving is extremely limited. They are used mainly in beveling.

I prefer and recommend the wheel most engravers prefer: the stone aluminum oxide wheel. This material simply works the best: it is durable, easily shaped, will hold its shape once it is formed (dressed) and will cut an unlimited number of design patterns, leaving a satin finish on the glass.

No wheels actually "come" with the engraving machine itself. Wheels must be purchased separately and, as noted above, must be dressed (shaped) by the engraver to his or her specifications before being used. I recommend buying at least four wheels initially to learn to dress the different shapes. I will go into the different wheels for different effects shortly.

Cost depends on the size of the wheel and its composition. Generally speaking diamond wheels cost the most, depending on whether they are bonded (an 8" x 1-1/2" x 1" 100 mesh might go for over $500) or electroplated (the same wheel would go for around $275). However a 6" x 1/2" x 1" stone wheel of aluminum oxide, which is the size I recommend, would only cost around $40 and will last a long time with extensive use. If you want to start with smaller wheels than that (you

Two wheels are shown, an olive wheel on the left and a mitre wheel on the right and both are riding on a pair of sponges. Having the sponge placed in this position is one way of making sure your wheel has enough water.

might want to get three just to form the three basic shapes) you can get some measuring 2" x 1/2" x 5/8" for $10 each. You can get smaller ones than that for less than half that price though I don't recommend it. Remember, these wheels will last for quite a long time and as long as you don't abuse them (drop them, run over them, use them as weapons), you'll get your money's worth in fun and pride of accomplishment.

How the Wheel Makes the Marks on the Glass

The wheel makes (according to the wheel shape you have created) specific marks on the

Showing wheels of different diameters, bushed and unbushed. Left is the printy, top center is the olive with the mitre below, and on the right is the strap wheel.

A bushed strap wheel.

An unbushed mitre wheel.

glass by you (the operator) pressing and turning the glass against the spinning wheel from above. Accordingly, the work is done on the under surface of the glass, the cutting surface of the wheel spinning and impressing the design as you go. You apply force to the wheel by the amount of pressure you put on the glass pressing against it; the more force you apply, the deeper the cut will be, therefore the more heat will be applied to the glass by friction. That's why you need water; it keeps the heat down.

You look through the glass from above, guiding the process. To temporarily halt the

proceedings, whether to consider the best way to continue the design or to wipe the glass from water spray so you can see better, just lift the glass away from the wheel. It's that simple. You don't have to stop the wheel itself unless you want to take a break or to change wheels.

Wheels - Mitre, Strap, Printy, and Olive

Although these wheels are covered in Chapter Five much more fully, it might be well at this point to briefly discuss some wheel

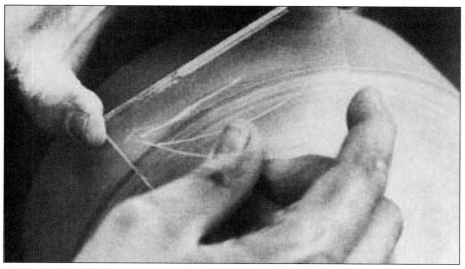

Using the strap wheel to cut lines. The strap wheel is used just as it comes from the factory. Note the way the glass is angled to use the sharp edge of the wheel to make the cut.

A typical engraved piece on a bevel lit from the front. This engraving used three wheels: a mitre, an olive, and a printy wheel.

Marks on glass made by the printy wheel.

Practice shapes on glass made by the mitre wheel.

More practice shapes on glass made by the mitre wheel. Note the wide variation.

These lines were made with the strap wheel.

Practice shapes on glass made by the olive wheel.

shapes. I have said that wheels come from the factory "undressed," that is with a standard flat edge. This edge must be transformed into a working engraving wheel. There are only a few ways to do this: rounding the edge to a greater or lesser extent, angling it to a smaller central square, or angling it more severely to a sharp pointed peak. The instrument used to do this is called a "dressing tool" and these are "sticks" made of silicon carbide or are diamond impregnated. I have never found it necessary to purchase the more expensive diamond variety. The use of the silicon carbide dressing stick is covered in Chapter Five.

Different shaped wheels. At lower left is a strap wheel, above it is a mitre wheel, and above and to the left of the mitre is an olive wheel. All these wheels have been bushed to take a tapered mandril. The bushing is the peculiar-looking center section that looks like a burst bubble.

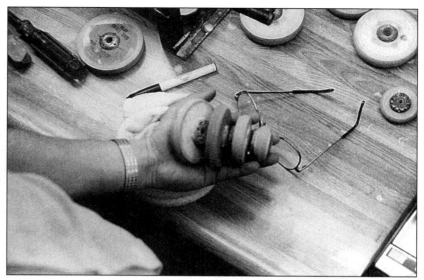

A further selection of wheels, all of which have been bushed. Note how many different sizes are available for use. Never, ever throw your old wheels away just because they have gotten smaller with use. Small wheels are precious in their own right.

The various shapes made on the glass have been given names for the wheels producing them. The number of different design formations the wheels can produce is not dependent on wheel shape but on the motion of the glass by the engraver over the turning wheel. It is important to keep this in mind. It is also true that wheel shapes can vary even within the same category of shape. Rounding the wheel edge to a certain extent will produce various sizes of olive wheel. This wheel will give the effect of an olive, a more or less oval shape.

A strap wheel, which is not changed from the way it comes from the factory, will produce a line like those seen in the photo on page 48.

Designs can be produced by turning the glass as the wheel is marking it and by varying the pressure. This is the technique of glass engraving that takes time to learn: how to twist and turn the glass for each individual wheel to get precisely the most out of it before having to change to differently shaped wheel. Each wheel must be manipulated according to the design you have in mind while keeping the pressure varied as to the depth of cut desired and also maintaining the proper flow of water. There's a lot going on at one time but you'll be surprised how fast your hands will begin to "sense" this engraving process.

When and How to Change Wheels

Obviously you don't want to spend all your time changing from one wheel to another so you should use each wheel to maximum effect before going on to the next. For instance, if you are doing three stalks of wheat, you wouldn't do a single curved line with the mitre wheel to indicate a stem, then change to the olive wheel to produce another part of the design, then change back to the mitre wheel to make the next stem. What you would do is make all three stems with the mitre wheel, then change to the olive wheel and make all those portions of the design pertaining to that wheel. Obviously, this calls for a proper laying out of the design before you begin to engrave. If you don't do this but just decide to "wing it" you'll be spending a lot of time not only changing your wheels but spinning them.

Shifts in the Wheel

I keep remarking that the axle must run absolutely true when it is turning. This is so important that it's advisable to check occasionally to make certain it is running true. If the wheel is really way off you'll be able to see this just by watching it. However if it is off just a bit you can check it in the following manner. Take a piece of scrap glass and hold the scrap glass against the wheel with equal pressure to make a cross and then check with a lens to see if the cuts are even in depth and equal in width and length..

If the two lines of the cross are not the same dimensionally, you can possibly tap the axle lightly with a hammer to a more precise motion of the wheel. However, the problem may not be with the axle. Unhappily, you can have an absolutely true axle and still have a wheel that whirls irregularly. Why? The problem may be in the wheel itself. There are two possible imperfections of motion to the wheel - bounce and wobble. Neither of these are hard to fix.

Bounce is an up and down imperfection that may be quite easy to spot or difficult to spot, depending on the degree of bounce present. Bounce occurs when the wheel is out of balance vertically. Bounce will occur if the center hole, whether bushed or open, is not perfectly aligned with the mandril. It will also occur if the wheel isn't tightened sufficiently. Be careful here, for if you over-tighten the wheel to try to get rid of bounce, you could crack it. It's best to hand tighten any wheel. Never, never use a wrench to tighten the nut on a straight threaded spindle. You can exert far too much pressure without realizing it until the wheel breaks in pieces. Besides that, a wrench is one more thing to have to reach for when changing wheels. Let's keep the process as simple and as efficient as possible. The first thing to try to alleviate bounce with a straight spindle is to see if the nut is loose. If it isn't, loosen it and try turning the wheel to another position on the spindle.

Wobble is a side-to-side motion that can occur with bounce or by itself. It is a discrepancy in horizontal balance. Wobble occurs when the wheel is out of line front to back, and is just as likely to happen with a straight as a tapered mandril.

Eliminating Bounce and Wobble

Every time you place a brand new wheel on the mandril, you will need to correct the wheel to eliminate bounce and wobble, regardless of whether you are using a straight mandril or a tapered mandril. It isn't a question of any misjudgment on your part, bounce and wobble come with the territory. It's critical that before you touch a piece of glass to your wheel, you have that wheel turning in as absolutely true a fashion as you can calculate by eye. By eye, especially for beginners, is usually good enough; you don't need any other measurement at this point unless you want to try the cross measurement described above. However, even that can be done away with while you are learning the basics. But if, by eye, your wheel is not true, your engraving will end up a good example of what bounce and wobble can look like in glass. An erratic collection of lines will occur because of loss of control of the wheel. Not exactly what you had in mind.

Any corrective process to the wheel should be done gradually. Correcting bounce first, then wobble is my standard procedure, though this is not written in stone. The important thing is not to try to correct both problems at once. If you do, you can literally end up going in circles, since you will have no basis upon which to measure one dimensional irregularity against the other. Most beginners try to correct bounce and wobble as a single entity and discover, as we all have, that it leads to misjudgment in all directions.

It's hard to say which of these erratic wheel situations is the worst. Either is frustrating and together they can appear at first glance to be insuperable. However, they are correctable and you do want to correct them, not ignore them since the more bounce and wobble your wheel possesses, the poorer your end result will be since the final engraved piece will be out of control. The good news is that both of these annoying wheel tendencies can be overcome, though it can take varying degrees of time and patience to do so as well as, unfortunately, waste of material. Correcting bounce and wobble will be covered in the next chapter; all you need know about it here is that these discrepancies exist and getting them under control is also part of the pre-engraving process.

Summary

Naturally, when you are engraving you don't want to spend half your time with the wheel changing operation. As an artist you really want to be occupied with the creative work. But you may as well realize now that your wheels must be precisely right from the start or the engraved glass won't have a chance at coming out as you visualize it.

As noted, I feel the straight mandril wastes too much time, not only with getting the nuts off and on and making sure they are tight but not too tight, but in the necessity of having to re-evaluate the balance each time the wheels are changed. I find I get much more bounce with the straight mandril than with the tapered mandril and spend less time with the tapered once the initial bushing has been accomplished. However, everyone works differently and it is certainly advantageous to realize there are two possibilities and to try each to find which type of mandril works best for you.

Much of this chapter may sound tangential, hardly what you might expect as far as glass working is concerned. At this point. I can almost hear you saying, "Hey, I want to engrave glass, not correct wheels." Alas, in any hand craft, one has to make a proper beginning in order to begin. You must learn the characteristics of the tools you need to use to turn out work you will be proud of. Once you do learn them, noting and correcting such characteristics will become second nature.

Chapter Four: Preparing the Wheel - The Bushing Process

As I mentioned earlier, I prefer the tapered mandril to the straight one as a means of supporting my engraving wheels. Using a tapered mandril requires that you complete the process called bushing. The word "bushing," as used in this instance, means filling the center hole in the wheel with material that will allow the wheel to securely fit onto a tapered mandril, since otherwise the hole would be too large. A special device called a casting table is necessary to accomplish this purpose. I will show you how to use a casting table later in the chapter.

If you do not wish to use a tapered mandril but want to employ only the straight variety, you won't have to bush your wheels. The straight mandril is made to fit the center wheel hole and the wheel will be held firmly by the nut and cup washer on the other side. By the way, make sure you always use the cup washer, as this takes up some of the strain on the wheel from tightening. The straight mandril may appear to be the easier procedure, as opposed to bushing and initially it is. However, as mentioned previously, you will then likely have to contend with a certain amount of wheel imbalance (bounce and wobble) every time you change wheels. This can be extremely annoying. The time you may have to spend correcting such imbalance may end up being more extensive than the bushing procedure. However, you

are certainly welcome to go the route of the straight mandril if you wish to try it first as opposed to the extra procedure of bushing. At the same time, bushing is kind of fun. Once you have learned how to use the casting table, you will find it a quick and easy process. After you

A propane torch and flame lighter.

have produced a set of bushed wheels, you need not repeat the procedure until and unless you add a new wheel.

What's Involved

The bushing process requires several items that you must acquire separately from the engraving machine: lead, a propane torch, a metal pan, and a casting table.

Lead is the material that is used to fill the center wheel hole. It is so employed because it is easily melted with just a propane torch, it solidifies rapidly and it is pliable enough to take the impression of the mandril's threads and strong enough to hold them firmly. It will also provide the proper stability to support the wheel during the engraving process. Lead is easy to get hold of and is inexpensive, two other characteristics that mark it as the material of choice.

A propane torch is easily acquired from your local hardware store. If you've never used one before, there's really nothing to it.

All you have to remember is to keep the nozzle pointed away from you and to turn it off immediately when you aren't using it. Don't let the flame continue to burn while you are engaged in some other project. Use a flint or gas lighter to light your torch, not matches, which bring your fingers too close to the flame.

You will need a metal pan of some sort in which to melt the lead. Any pan will do that won't itself melt when you apply the torch. An old frying pan works well. The pan needn't be large and certainly shouldn't be unwieldy since you will have to lift it to pour the molten lead. You may want to use an oven mitt or pliers to handle the pan, which will get hot.

The Casting Table

The casting table is an essential part of the bushing procedure. It is a small table with a flat circular top the surface of which is ring-calibrated to allow you to place your wheel

A casting table. Note the concentric rings on top. These are guides to place various sizes of wheels for bushing so as to keep the center hole in the center.

precisely in the center. The hole in the wheel will fit right over the center hole of the casting table, through which the mandril will protrude. The casting table holds the mandril for you and allows you to place the wheel on it so that precisely the amount of mandril you wish to have protruding from the wheel will do so. I will go over this procedure in depth a little further on. You can purchase a casting table at the same time you buy your engraving machine. Prices vary, of course, but $200 should get you one or you can try purchasing a used one on the Internet.

It is important to keep in mind that a wheel, once it is lead bushed, will be individualized to the specific mandril to which it has been molded. No other mandril, regardless how much it may look exactly like the one the bushing was made for, should be substituted for the original one. The delicate threading in the lead bushing imparted by the mandril as the molten lead flows around it particularizes the fit to a specific mandril. Discrepancies between mandrils are always present even though each may look to be tapered to the same degree. Such discrepancies, if a second mandril is forced into a bushing made for another mandril, will ruin the bushing and throw the wheel off. The lead will then have to be melted out of the wheel and the entire bushing procedure will have to be redone.

As a beginner it is unlikely that you will acquire more than one tapered mandril, but just in case you have an extra one hanging around, make sure you mark the one you will use for each wheel and only use that one.

To re-specify: Once the wheels are bushed to fit a tapered mandril, even though the bushing can move somewhat, you have wheels that are 99% molded to that mandril. This means a particular wheel will always go back on the mandril the same way it came

off; that it will fit precisely the way it did last time, with no extra fuss. If such a wheel was true the first time, it will be true the second, third, and fourth times unless it is severely stressed in some manner - as by a forceful drop or by being over-tightened or bent while on the mandril.

Bushing Your Own Wheels

Some workers are fearful of the bushing process. Some even take their wheels to metal workers to have them bushed. I bush my own wheels and advise you to do the same. The process is part of engraving. There is some equipment involved, but nothing ornate or expensive. Of course, if you really aren't interested in this process, you can send the wheel out to be bushed, but if you do, you must also send the mandril you intend to use with each wheel. Even though these mandrils are machined to exact specifications, if you take a wheel from one machine and put it on a mandril from another machine, you could get a little bounce. In all likelihood you would have to re-bush the wheel.

It's not just because you'll spend less money that it's best to bush your own wheels. If you are going to take engraving seriously, you can't keep sending wheels out. Too much time and effort is wasted. Most frustrating about not doing the job yourself is getting a wheel back that still has wobble or bounce and must go back to be re-bushed. No one handles your necessities as well as you do.

Roughing the Hole

The first step in bushing the wheel is to get the center hole ready to accept the molten lead you will pour into it. When the wheel comes from the factory, the center hole is smoothly machined. You don't want that, for

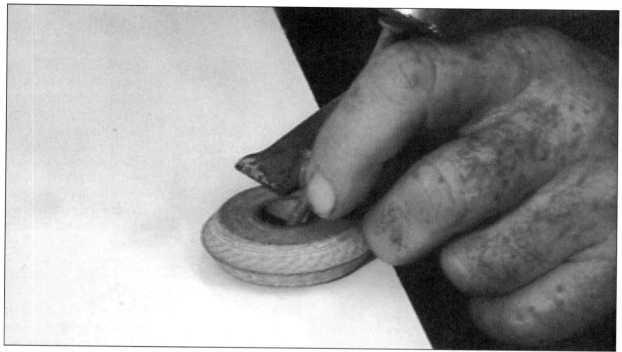

Roughing a mitre wheel for bushing. Here I'm using a long nail which I'm tapping with a hammer. Note the edge of the clamp holding the wheel behind my two fingers that are holding the nail. Clamping the wheel to the table makes it unable to move and so makes the roughing operation easier and safer.

if you allow it to stay that way, the lead will slip around on this smooth surface, having no purchase.

I overcome this by chipping out a pattern into the smooth center of the wheel that will allow the lead to grab. Always use safety glasses when chipping; you will find the bits and pieces of the wheel material flying about. Always clamp the wheel you are working on to the table with a C-clamp. Never attempt to chip a wheel that is not firmly held down. The reasons for this are obvious, but there is always the temptation to get things done without taking the time for proper precautions.

Chipping involves both sides of the wheel hole. You can actually chip all the way through the hole if you have a chisel small enough to fit. If not, turn the wheel over and chip the hole on the other side. The object is to make grooves, not to ream out the hole so it becomes larger; if you do ream out the hole you'll be buying a new wheel. Never chip all the way around the circle because that will create the very situation you are trying to overcome.

I use a chisel and hammer and chip four or five grooves in the center hole opposite one another. It's not brain surgery. You can substitute a large nail for the chisel if you wish. Chip downward directly into the hole at an extreme angle. If you chip straight down, the lead will not grip as well. You don't want to give that bushing the slightest opportunity to shift. Also, when chipping straight down, you are more apt to crack the wheel with the amount of force that is generated. These wheels, while very strong, are also quite brittle.

You can use a chisel or large nail to rough the hole. The operator is chipping what will be one of several grooves in the center hole. Unless this is done, the lead won't have anything to grab onto and the bushing will spin around in the center area, doing no good at all. Hold the chisel at a slant to prevent breaking the wheel.

Another method of roughing the center hole is with a glass saw blade, the kind that fits in a hacksaw handle. You don't need the handle; use the blade by itself to saw grooves in the center hole. Such a saw is fast and safe. While it tends to raise a small amount of dust, this is quite heavy and usually falls away, remaining in the air only a short time. An advantage to the saw is that it puts a consistent groove all the way through the center hole and makes a neat looking result.

Once you have chipped (or grooved) the wheel to your satisfaction, mark the position

If you hold the chisel straight up and down on the wheel, you'll end up with a broken wheel. There's not much you can do with pieces like this. The wheel will withstand many kinds of shocks but not direct blows to the surface.

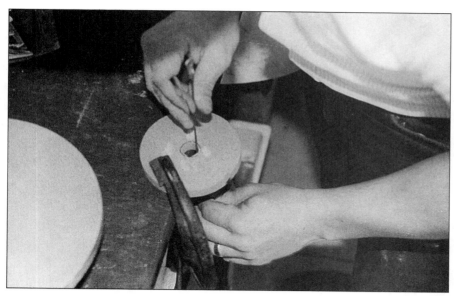

Another way to acquire purchase for the lead bushing is to groove out the inner hole with a glass saw blade. The wheel must be stabilized against the table with some sort of clamp and at least three grooves must be sawed into the center hole at least 1/8" deep. Whether you use a saw blade or chip with a chisel, remember to mark the location of the grooves with pencil lines on the outer surface of the wheel.

of each of the grooves on the flat side of the wheel. Draw a pencil line from each groove as a firm indication of where the grooves have been placed. You will see why shortly. Then clean up the area and set your wheel into position for bushing.

How Much Mandril Should Protrude?

Since the mandril is tapered, you can theoretically put as much or as little of it through the hole as you wish. Normally about 1/4 of the threading can be seen coming out the far end of the bushing with a small-to-medium size wheel. For a large wheel, placement should be farther back on the mandril for strength (and thus have a considerable quantity of taper coming through the hole). The amount of protruding mandril shouldn't get in the way of hand motions because the circumference of the wheel keeps the action away from the excess taper.

On the other hand, you will want to place a small wheel close to the end of the mandril (with very little taper coming through). Hand motion in this instance is very close to the mandril. If you run a small or medium wheel all the way up the mandril, you end up with a lot of taper protruding, which will get in your way when you attempt to make engraving motions holding the glass. There must be as much free space as possible to maneuver the glass. You don't want to keep hitting on that impinging mandril when you're concentrating all your powers on getting the design engraved.

As a rule of thumb, when bushing a small wheel, bush it practically to the end of the mandril, with almost no taper coming through. The bigger the wheel, the more you run it up the taper for stability. With really large wheels, the circumference of the wheel protects the glass from hitting whatever taper is coming through the bushing. Obviously, it would be foolish to attempt to balance a large wheel on the tip of the mandril. In such a case there wouldn't be

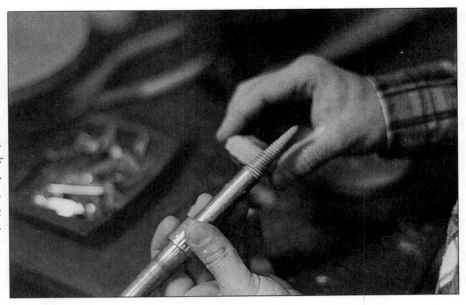

Measuring where you want the unbushed wheel to be in its final position on the tapered mandril. This small wheel has been purposely placed too far back on the mandril. If positioned this way, the front portion of the mandril would interfere with the hand motion necessary to engraving.

enough grip for stability and the whole balance of the engraving machine would probably be awry.

Sealing the Center Hole of the Casting Table

After you decide how much of the tapered mandril you wish to have protruding through the wheel, try the wheel on the casting table, with the mandril coming through the center hole. You will note that when the tapered mandril is in the center hole of the casting table it has a lot of space around it. This gap cannot be allowed to remain, since once you place the wheel on the table and start pouring lead, the lead will pour right through the casting table. You must seal this area. There are a number of seals that can be used: aluminum foil is a good choice, but anything compressible that doesn't combine with the molten lead should be all right to use.

Fill this space between the mandril and the table fully and completely so that the filler material comes level to the surface of the casting table. Remember, now, we're talking about the casting table, not the wheel. We haven't placed the wheel back on the table as yet. When the wheel is placed back on the table, there shouldn't be any part of the center hole in the casting table for the lead to flow into. It will, therefore, only fill the hole in the wheel and not any part of the hole in the table.

I find a most effective filler is gasket material, available at auto shops. I break off a piece and plug the gap with it. I first work it in with my fingers, then augment what my fingers have done with a flat surface tool like a chisel or screwdriver. Even a pencil will do - anything that can get into the crevice and pack the material down.

With the center gap of the table sealed and the mandril in place, you are ready to place your wheel back on the table, making sure it fits directly along one of the concentric table rings. In this manner it will be directly centered.

The metal solid shaft fits in the hole of the casting table to allow various sizes of tapered spindles to go to various depths, depending on how much taper the worker wishes to protrude from the hole. Some spindles are long enough so they don't need this shaft. They can be guided as to depth by the turnkey at the bottom of the table which will allow them to be raised or lowered as it is loosened or tightened.

Lowering the tapered spindle into the casting table from above.

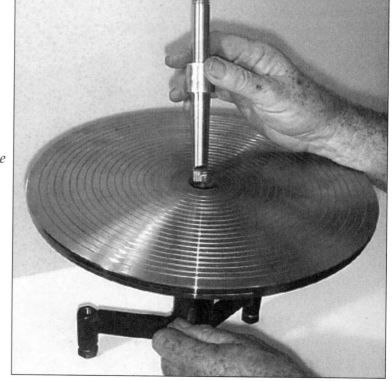

The casting table with the tapered spindle in place.

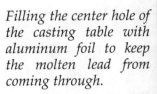

Filling the center hole of the casting table with aluminum foil to keep the molten lead from coming through.

The center hole filled to the top, leaving no opening around the projecting tapered spindle for the lead to get through.

Because the molten lead will spill over the top of the wheel hole to an extent, it's a good idea to make a little dam around that surface to contain this lead. The dam doesn't have to be extensive; about what is shown in the picture should suffice. This one is made of coiled aluminum foil.

Melting the Lead

To melt the lead, I recommend putting fairly small lead pieces into some type of melt pan - anything with a higher melting temperature than lead. An old frying pan will do (one that is not nonstick). You can acquire scrap pieces of lead from your plumber (plumb means lead) or a stained glass studio that is making leaded windows. Lead sinkers for fishing poles are available at sport shops and are inexpensive and easy to melt down. An aluminum cake pan will also do as an available and inexpensive melt pan. For safety measures make sure whatever melt pan you select has a flat bottom with no holes and that you are on a surface that is absolutely flat and doesn't rock. You don't want to lead bush the floor or your socks.

You must have a way to support the wheel in a horizontal (flat) position, and you must be able to calculate the length of the mandril, which must come up through the center hole to just the proper height and must be abso-

Placing the mandril from below. The casting table is the larger circle under my hand upside down. The mandril is being placed in the casting table, which has been turned upside-down to allow the procedure. The objective is to have just the right portion of the mandril tip emerge from the bushed wheel.

Here is the casting table seen from the top with the mandril coming through the center hole. Note the concentric rings in the casting table - they serve as guidelines for placing the wheel.

lutely perpendicular to the surface. All these requirements are most readily accomplished with a lead casting table as discussed previously. The casting table is specific for casting lead centers (bushings) in stone wheels to prepare for engraving. It allows for easy removal and perfect centering on tapered spindles. Such a table, with its round top and concentric circles, will make sure the spindle is properly centered. Such tables may be purchased from the Denver Glass Machinery Co. and will last indefinitely. You might try mak-

From the top you can see the space surrounding the tapered point of the mandril. This space must be filled in or the molten lead used as bushing will come through it. I use gasket material or aluminum foil to fill it.

ing one yourself since it looks simple enough, but by the time you have just the metal top cut and polished and calibrated by your local engineer, you will probably be over-costing what one complete will cost from the manufacturer (about $200).

The casting table holds the mandril from below at a precise perpendicular angle to the top bed on which the wheel will lay. The wheel and mandril are placed so that as the lead is poured, the lead will be the only thing that moves. Of course, if you pour it so it dribbles on your shoes, you may be doing some moving yourself.

You must do your best to get a perfect fit when bushing. There are a number of ways wheels can go out of sync after the bushing process. If they go off during the process, it can be downhill all the way. The melting and pouring process is therefore critical.

Some workers light the propane torch by simply turning on the gas and holding a match to the end of the regulator. I prefer the flame lighter shown on page 52.

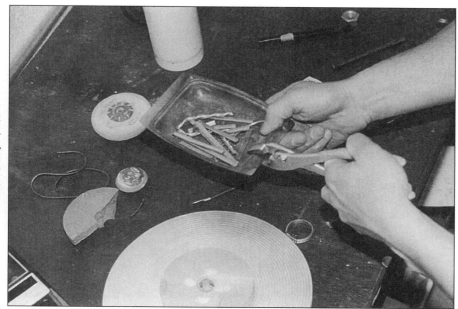

Place pieces of scrap lead in a container that can withstand the heat you will be applying. Since the pan will get hot, grip it with pliers or an oven mitt, never with your bare hand.

Using a standard propane torch to melt your lead (not the kitchen stove) and remembering to use an oven mitt if you have to handle the melt pan, pass the flame of the torch over the pieces of lead. It doesn't take long before you will see the globules of lead begin to form. I use a pair of pliers to hold the pan since I find oven mitts awkward but I advise you not to use pliers for

The torch starts to melt the lead almost as soon as the heat is applied. Lead has a very low melting point.

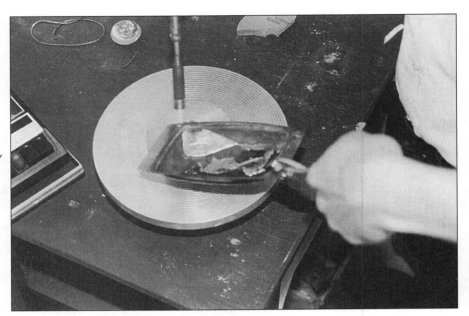

The lead, in molten state, is beginning to puddle.

this purpose unless you are used to handling them. I always keep my melt pan close to the table top, not in mid air and away from my body so if the pan falls I don't get spattered with lead. Some people prefer to do their melting outdoors. Depending on the temperature and the weather you may find it will take longer to melt the lead outdoors. Remember, you don't need to incinerate the lead; just melt it sufficiently to come up with a nice pool of material.

If the lead smokes as it's melting, it's likely that there's some solder or other foreign material mixed with the scrap lead. Don't panic. As soon as the non-lead material burns out, the smoke will stop.

I don't advise melting lead on a stove burner. The stove is in the kitchen and usually there is food around. Food and lead do not go together; lead oxides are not what you want to take into your body. On the other hand, you don't need to wear a mask when melting lead. If fumes arise because of impurities in the lead, obviously you don't want to breathe these in, but such fumes don't last long.

How much lead do you use? Use more than enough to do the job, especially because you can't do two pourings. You have to get it right the first time or start over. That means always melt more lead than you think you will need. Should you come up short and try making a second pouring, your first pour will fill up the bottom of the hole in the wheel, and create the bottom of the bushing and your second pouring will create the top. Where the two surfaces meet will be a juncture, not a continuum. That means they will not have melded together but will be two separate areas that will move individually, making the bushing worthless.

Usually heating the lead will create a smokeless, molten pool. If smoke forms, this means you are heating some foreign material as well. Solder mixed in with the lead will cause smoke. Scrap lead is not necessarily pure lead; if you get your lead from a stained glass studio, some pieces of solder may be mixed in with it. You may not realize this until the lead begins to smoke. Smoke does not necessarily indicate a serious problem, though you should not breathe it. Wave it away. Keep heating the material and the foreign matter will eventually be burned up. It's good to know about the possibility of smoke and make sure, before you begin melting the lead, that you are in a well ventilated work area.

Pouring the Lead

Before you pour the molten lead, you need to correctly position the wheel on the casting table if you haven't already done so. The wheel can't be placed on the table just any old way. The casting wheel has a number of concentric rings on it, which are there to help you center the stone wheel. It is essential that the wheel be centered and it's simple to do. Line

The wheel to be bushed is placed on the casting table precisely centered using the concentric rings on the casting table as a guide. The amount of mandril coming through is exactly right.

To keep the surplus of molten lead from running over the wheel, place a small catch ring or dam around the center hole. If you work in stained glass and have lead came on hand, use a small piece. Otherwise, you can use aluminum foil or any other material that won't melt.

up the wheel with one of the rings. Then, to make sure the lead doesn't over-pour all over the place as the wheel hole fills, make a little dam with a coil of gasket material or silver foil or anything that won't melt. The circumference of this coil only has to cover an area 1/2" or so larger than that of the center wheel hole. Make sure it is firmly in place. You shouldn't need any more room than that, but you should have at least that much because you want enough excess molten lead to spill out from the center hole to fill just this amount of space.

Keep the torch on the lead until just before pouring. The lead cools and hardens very quickly, so you need to keep it molten until all is poured in the hole.

Pouring the lead into the center hole.

This will allow the lead to cap the hole and maintain the bushing.

Once you're ready to carefully pour the molten lead, make sure you have plenty of room. Pour the lead in slowly until it comes up through the hole, just enough to spread out and cap off the bushing into that little space you have left for it. The lead cools almost instantly and that's how fast you are ready to work the wheel which is now firmly attached to the mandril.

Actually, the bushing may be all too firmly attached to the mandril Once the lead has cooled you may find it hard to de-thread the

The newly poured bushing in the center of the wheel on the casting table. See the calculated overflow of the bushing within the catch ring.

Once the molten lead is poured and allowed to harden, remove the wheel from the casting table. It may take a bit of turning to get the newly-bushed wheel to release from the mandril but it will come off eventually. This wheel is now bushed specifically for this mandril and should not be used with any other mandril.

mandril, that is to spin it out of the lead bushing - which is your next step. You may have to try several times to force the newly-bushed wheel off the mandril. Don't be alarmed, this is not out of the ordinary. Grasp the mandril with your fingers, holding it with a towel or something similar that will provide purchase (not a wrench) and twist at the wheel with your other hand. It may take several minutes and a good deal of force to feel the wheel loosening, but it will come off the mandril eventually; just have patience and keep twisting.

The Newly-Bushed Wheel

The newly bushed wheel will be hot in the center, but the outside will certainly be cool enough to handle. You can't immediately start to work it, but the first step in actually working up to the engraving process is done.

One problem that can occur, despite the roughing grooves in the center hole, is that while the molten lead takes up all the space allowed for it, once it cools it may shrink

away from those nice grooves you took such trouble to create. If that happens, the bushing will become loose. It won't actually spin around because the grooves prevent that, but it will (or may) wobble or bounce because it is loose. You will know it when you go to

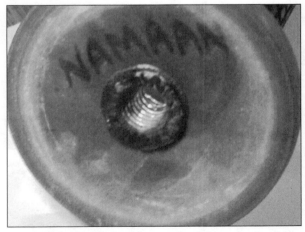

A bushed strap wheel lets us look into the bushing to see the threads that the tapered spindle has formed when the lead was melted around it.

The bushed wheel going onto the tapered mandril.

The bushed wheel screwed onto the tapered mandril, Note the amount of taper protruding beyond the wheel. This is a small wheel; a larger one would be situated further back with more mandril protruding for better stability.

work with it because such wheels will make a terrible noise.

How can you compensate for this frustrating development? There is no way to pour more lead in or hope to fill that shrinkage area because you won't even know it exists until the process is complete and you try the wheel. The probability of this occurring is at least 50%; the discrepancy is inherent in the nature of the bushing material.

Don't despair. Remember those pencil marks you made on the wheel to show where the grooves were cut? They will come in very handy now.

To make the shrunken bushing fit back into the grooves so the wheel runs smoothly, you have to tap it with a hammer. This may sound rather alarming for, if you recall, I mentioned that these wheels are strong but also somewhat fragile. So you don't want to slam it, and certainly not just anywhere. Follow each pencil line back to its groove and give this portion of the bushing a smart rap. This will usually compress that portion of the lead back into its groove. You may have

to tap a couple of times, each time re-trying the wheel.

I tap all wheels routinely after the bushing process. I don't want the hassle of getting the wheel ready to use and then having to go back and compress the lead because of a loose bushing. It's more reasonable and less time-wasting to do it right away. You must do this with the mandril in place, however. Otherwise when you hit the lead it will fill up part of the space taken up by the mandril as well as the groove you are trying to fill. Keeping the mandril in the bushing maintains the proper hole shape and as the lead is compressed, the mandril acts as a barrier to push it back into the wheel grooves. Give really solid taps. Don't be afraid of breaking the wheel since the lead absorbs the impact. And remember not to just whack the thing at random; aim for where the grooves are marked. Hitting the bushing in other areas will not do the job properly.

You can, if you wish, also hit the bushing on the bottom surface. I don't recommend this because this is not a stable area, since you

There are times when the bushing just doesn't work and must be remelted to flow out of the center hole. The torch is just starting to melt the lead out of the wheel.

More lead flows out of the bushing as the heating progresses.

can't remove the mandril and the shank will get in the way of your aim. Just tapping the bushing on the top side of the wheel where the taper protrudes should be sufficient. It's not as awkward as it sounds. Just grip the wheel by the mandril and hold that portion

of it you are going to tap over the worktable and give that top surface what for. Need I say that it's a good idea not to overdo this? You can smack the wheel around to such an extent that you actually malform the lead. If that happens, or if the lead has shrunk so

The remelted lead from the almost completely melted bushing is filling the little pan. No harm done - the remelted lead can be used over and the wheel hasn't been harmed. Note the lines on the surface of the wheel indicating where the grooves were cut.

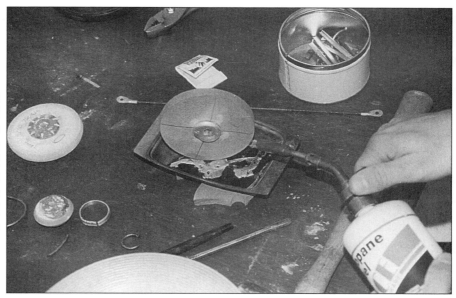

badly no amount of tapping the grooves will help, you just have to melt the lead back out of the wheel and start all over.

While this is annoying, no harm has been done. You can't hurt the wheel by the process of remelting the lead, since these wheels have already been fired in production. Certainly don't consider that you have to throw away any wheel simply because you have to redo its bushing. That's not true and would certainly be a waste. Redoing a bushing may cost you some time but nothing in the way of materials. Think of it as a learning process.

Once the wheel has been properly bushed it is ready for dressing (shaping). We're getting closer now to finalizing the pre-engraving process and going into the actual engraving process. Stay with it.

Chapter Five: Preparing the Wheel - The Dressing Process

Purchasing Wheels Already Dressed

To a certain extent, already dressed wheels are available but these are diamond wheels. For use with the EG-1 engraver, the "V" wheel and "printy" wheel can be purchased from the Denver Glass Machinery Co. and these wheels will produce many of the basic lines and shapes used in the engraving process should you want to be locked into only basic shapes. These wheels run approximately $100 apiece for sizes from 4" x 1/8" x 1/2" to 4" x 1/4" x 1/2". Compare this to a stone wheel of comparable size that costs approximately $20.

The reason stone wheels do not come already dressed certainly involves cost (they would cost a lot more) but also because engraving is a very individual process. There is no way a manufacturer would be able to produce dressed wheels that an engraver wouldn't be modifying for his/her own use anyway. And while it's true there are only so many basic shapes, the amount of modifications of these shapes for each individual engraver's demands would defeat any mass production basis. It's much simpler all around for the wheel manufacturer to provide the basic wheel and let you, the artist, shape it to your needs.

Checking the Wheel

After you have bushed your wheel, you need to know if you are going to have any problems with it running true and if so how extensive these problems are. Problems can vary from the readily fixable to the absolutely unusable. You may have done everything absolutely right and still end up with wobble or bounce. But that's life.

So the first thing to do is place the newly bushed wheel in the engraving machine and watch how it turns. Even if the wheel runs reasonably well, it's still not good enough to engrave a piece of glass. However, any small discrepancy can be fixed.

Check for high points (bounce) by placing a pen or pencil (pencil is what I have found best) on a solid brace and, holding it against the turning wheel, run a mark parallel to the wheel rim on the turning surface. This mark should stay equidistant from the rim if the wheel is turning evenly. If it is not, if the wheel is bouncing to any extent and thus producing a high point, the pencil line will vary in that area. If there is wobble, the wheel will veer away from the pencil in that area and there will be a skip in the line. This simple test will indicate discrepancies.

Any high spots can be touched up but this should be done right away. To remove high

Use a pen or pencil to mark high points on the wheel. Hold the pen steady (the support bar helps) and barely touch the pen to the wheel. Don't do this with the water on.

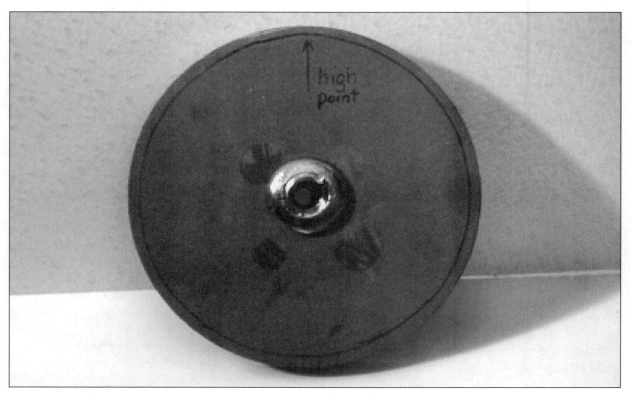

A newly-bushed wheel marked with a pencil to show a high spot. This must be ground down with a dressing stone or a grinding wheel.

Remove high points with a grinding wheel. Take care not to take off too much of the wheel beyond the high point. Hold the wheel firmly when applying it to the grinder and check the guidelines carefully and often.

spots from bounce you can use a grinding wheel or a hand-held silicon carbide stick available from your engraving supplier. A grinding wheel is best if you have one (a dremel tool or a hand piece will hold a satisfactory grinding wheel) since even with the bushed wheel as steady as you can get it and the silicon carbide stick held firmly, this process is not always accurate. However, if the touchup is minor, you may not have to use the grinder; you can hold the stick firmly in your hands and use the strength created by your arms in that working triangle I spoke of earlier. Remember to use your elbow pads, even if all you do is touchup, and make sure you wear protective eye glasses.

Whatever you do, don't use a chisel to get off high points. I've seen people try it. Such a procedure will quickly chip and ruin the wheel.

If the wheel suffers from wobble, you can tap against it while it's turning to try to straighten it out. This can be tedious and the tendency among beginners is to over-compensate by tapping too hard. This will merely produce more wobble. It takes a bit of practice, but you will quickly learn just

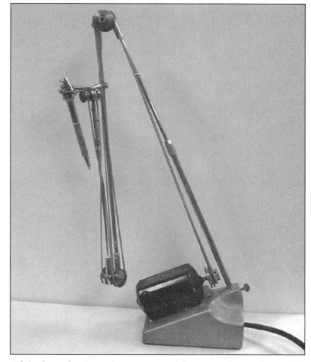

This hand piece is comparable to a dremel tool (I prefer the hand piece). The base is solid and I find the working end easier to hold in my hand than the bulkier dremel tool. Both will accomplish the same purpose. The end of the hand piece unscrews to allow the bit to be inserted.

Grinding the high points off a wheel using a grinding stone held in the hand piece. You want to go slowly here so you don't take off too much of the wheel you are grinding.

how hard to tap. Please keep in mind that I am exaggerating the amount of problems you may have with the newly-bushed wheel. Don't throw up your hands and toss your engraving machine out the window. In many cases such discrepancies will be minor and readily fixed. I am merely noting some of the more radical possibilities.

Tapping the wheel with a silicon carbide stick to correct wobble. The wheel must be turning very slowly to correct this discrepancy and multiple tappings may be necessary before the wheel will run true. If you tap too hard, you will over-compensate and take that much longer to get it right.

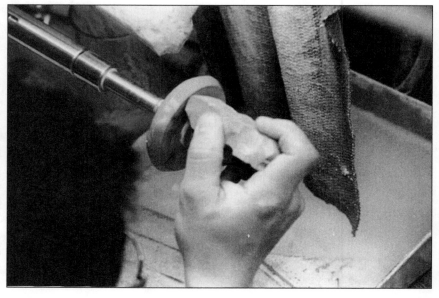

Here the wheel to be dressed is mounted on the engraving machine and I'm pressing the dressing stick against it. Notice how the stick is supported by the bar.

Correcting Bounce As Opposed to Getting Rid of High Points

Unfortunately you can't begin to shape the wheel until it is running absolutely true. You can't go to step C before step A is completed. Only when there is no discernible wobble or bounce or any other reason for a discrepancy can you go on to the next step, which is dressing (shaping) the wheel. Most wobble and bounce corrections as noted are often a matter of tapping the wheel while it is running. This can bring a slightly off-balanced wheel into line. Such a procedure won't work for removing high points, which are actual defects of the wheel's surface and can only be removed by grinding them away. So touch up high spots with a silicon carbide stick or a grinding wheel. If even a grinder cannot get rid of the high point problem, or no manner of tapping the wheel will get rid of wobble or bounce, you will probably have to re-bush the wheel. Sometimes it's better to bite the bullet and re-bush right away than attempt to modify a totally erratic wheel. If you spend more than an hour attempting to get a wheel running true, you would be better off re-bushing it.

Dressing Raw Wheels

Stone engraving wheels come from the manufacturer in "raw" form. Such wheels are still raw even after the bushing process. Before they can be properly used for engraving, they must be shaped to the desired form to do the various cuts on the glass surface that you want to impose. Let me stress once again that dressing the wheel, like dressing yourself, is strictly an individual process. Dressing the wheel involves grinding stone off the flat rim the wheel comes with to create a particular shape of cutting surface that will impart a specific imprint to the glass.

To do the necessary grinding, you need a silicon carbide dressing stick, 120 grit. That is the only type you will need for stone wheels. This inexpensive item is available from your engraving supplier for around $10. The dressing bar is something you will have to fiddle together yourself. Any arrangement that provides two legs and a center support will do. You can use pieces of pipe or portions of the steel standards that support metal shelving. Such standards have screw holes and go together quite easily. You employ these items by holding the stick in your hands against the wheel as it turns. To hold the stick steady, you support it on the dressing support bar. The dressing process is very similar to turning wood on a lathe. As the wheel turns, the pressure of the dressing stick against it grinds away stone, leaving a profile in the stone that will impart a shape to the glass in the specific pattern you desire.

Dressing the wheel can be somewhat messy. The proper quantity of water must be used to keep the procedure from getting out of hand and wrecking the wheel you have so carefully bushed. Since water tends to spatter, always wear safety glasses. Adjusting the water to the proper drip is crucial. Since you remove a considerable amount of stone from the wheel to shape it properly, it is necessary to have a sufficient quantity of water coming down over the wheel while you're grinding the stone off. This is where a pressure water system beats one that is merely gravity fed. Not enough water means there will be a great amount of stone dust in the air, and inhaling such dust over a period of time can lead to health problems. There is absolutely no problem, however, if you keep the water flowing. The water turns the dust into a clay that falls safely into the drip pan. Because dressing the wheel is a grinding process that creates dust, take precautions both to keep the dust down with a good supply of water, and to wear a face mask just in case some dust gets into the air. Glass artisans have been doing this procedure for years with no ill effects, but have taken the necessary precautions.

Once you learn to adjust the water to do its job without giving you more of a job cleaning up excess spray and once you get used to the overall procedure, dressing the wheel will become just another part of your routine. All the same, it can be awkward the first few times.

When everything is set - water, light, height, stance, pressure - and after you've decided what shape you want, you will begin to shape the wheel. Need I mention that the wheel should be running? Well, it should be. There is no mold to put over the wheel to help you get the right shape, nor is there any sort of template to measure against to see if the shape is true. You go strictly by eye. If you make a mistake, you just work it away and keep on toward your basic shape. There is enough wheel material to work with so don't get distressed if you have to waste some of it making

Dressing the wheel means shaping it for the engraving procedure, since wheels come from the manufacturer with flat surfaces. To apply the necessary pressure on the wheel, you need a strong support for the grinding stick. While you will hold the dressing stick firmly in your hands, you aren't strong enough to hold it completely steady for any length of time. The bar in front of the drip tray is the dressing support bar. Ideally, the drip tray would fit between the two support pillars, but positioning the tray behind the bar works fine too.

up for errors. Of course, you don't want to get it wrong too many times; then you will be wasting time and material. Once your wheel is dressed, it is ready to be used to engrave. You don't have to seal it or spray it.

Stone wheel engraving is one of the most satisfying crafts that I know and the small amount of preparation and control of materials that it requires to work properly and safely is, as you will see, a small measure to pay for so spectacular a return. The water supply is the key and a successful wheel production requires it to vary from a drip to a trickle to a steady pour during wheel dressing.

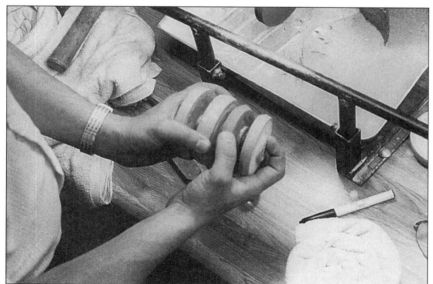

Four raw wheels. Their rounded surfaces are flat and must be dressed for engraving.

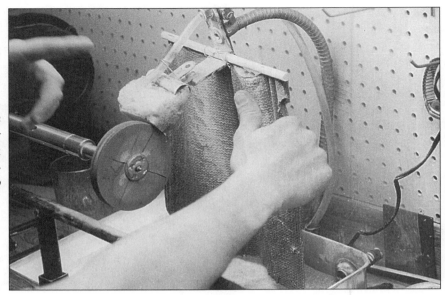

Preparing to dress the wheel. The raw bushed wheel is mounted on the engraving machine, the sponge is in place, and the dressing support bar is in position (below my arm).

Let's look at this process of dressing a little more closely. The dressing bar is designed to hold the dressing stick stable. The support bar, composed of two legs and a resting surface should be close to the wheel and slightly below half its circumference. Once the bar is in the correct position, it can be screwed to the table to hold it steady. To allow for this, make sure the legs have screw holes. If you are using portions of steel shelving standards, such screw holes already exist. You can make a square of these pieces and screw the lower portion to the table. Whatever you use for a dressing bar, it must be solid. You are going to be putting a lot of pressure against the wheel with the dressing stick, and

Dressing the wheel begins. A great deal of pressure can be applied to the wheel using the support bar. Here the wheel is being shaped from the bottom.

Here the wheel is being shaped from the top. Notice how the hand position changed.

for this reason, as well as making a correct dressing, you want everything sturdy.

The dressing stick should rest about halfway up (or down) the wheel. If it is too high or too low it will be awkward to use. There's no set rule as to exactly where to place the dressing stick except if it is too high you won't be able to see what's going on and will end up working in the blind. You need to be able to see the space between the stone and the stick. You can best see the stone and its contact with the dressing stick when the stick is held low.

Controlling Water Flow

Let me again state: Nothing should be done to the wheel without an adequate amount of water flowing over its surface. A sponge is the tried and true reservoir for water used to lubricate a wheel (as in a grinder). The sponge is held to its stand by a clip of some sort. It needn't be a real sponge - all you need is something that will absorb water, hold it, then disperse it over the stone. You can't do without this water reservoir because you will never be able to get the water to flow directly onto the stone effectively.

Though the sponge has to come in contact with the stone, it shouldn't be rammed into it. Merely having the sponge touch the stone is enough. You can tell if it's not touching sufficiently if the water sprays your face. In this case, the sponge will fill with water then drip directly onto the turning wheel, which will create spray back at you.

I hang a small piece of waterproof material behind the sponge to act as a "shower" curtain to protect the wall or the back of the worktable. The motion of the wheel is counterclockwise, which means that it turns towards you.

Shapes of the Wheel

Surprisingly few basic shapes are needed to be able to engrave a wide range of impressions in glass. But don't let this fool you. There are numerous modifications of these wheel shapes. However, let's consider the four wheel profiles you will dress your raw wheels into. With these four wheels as a start, you can engrave just about any design.

Why different shaped wheels? Why not just one shape? Well, each shaped wheel will make a different impression in the glass. It's a combination of these impressions that makes the design you have in mind. Just as in painting, where there are different brushes for different strokes, there are there different shaped wheels. Each wheel will cut into the glass differently and you change wheels to combine these particular cuts. At the same time, it isn't any of these four basic shapes that makes a good engraver. Each wheel will act upon the glass in its own way for anyone who goes through the practice of using it. It's what you do with these shapes to impose upon the glass your particular aesthetic that makes the artist in glass. The ideal is to learn the basics of what each shaped wheel will do, and then create and re-create with them. However, this is something no book can teach you; it's something you really learn by practice.

You will never be able to do much with any wheel shape to make it terribly innovative on its own. You can modify any of the four basic wheel shapes to make it cut a longer or shorter, thicker or thinner impression in glass. It's the decisions you make that involve those combinations of shapes from all four wheels. This depends on your imagination and your skill in maneuvering the glass on the particular wheel of your choice. This end result may appear so lovely, so skilled, and so complex that it's almost magical, but in reality it will be the result of many hours of experimenting.

The olive wheel makes an olive-shaped cut.

The Olive Wheel

The profile for this wheel is a slight curve and the cut it makes is literally an olive shape.

You shape the wheel so it has a slight convexity to its surface rather than the flat surface of the raw wheel. You can have different thicknesses of olive wheels to make different sized cuts; in fact you can have quite a number of modifications of all the different wheels, though you have to be careful not to overdo this. Learn to use the basic shapes before you start individualizing them. The basic olive shape is an elongated circle, an oval but with a deep center. By reworking that single shape, either with different sized olive wheels or by varied hand motions such as tipping side to side or front to back, you can produce a large number of different images in the glass. So, in addition to what the wheel will cut by itself, the shape can be modified by various engraving motions with your hands. You can pull the shape, twist it, mottle it, use it to add detail to a face, do a realistic rendition of a mouse sitting on a branch, etc.

It may seem obvious to say so, but complicated designs are merely collections of geometrics: circles and ovals and lines modified with skids and slopes and twists and drags, the hand motions that transform these movements and cuts into jeweled creations. Shapes can be done quickly and handily, just popping them into the glass as collections of geometric patterns.

The Mitre Wheel

The mitre wheel has a point running down its center. Its two sides, therefore, flare off a central raised portion. That flare can vary from a slight taper to one so extreme that the wheel becomes almost a disk. I occasionally use an extreme mitre wheel (one that is prac-

The mitre wheel makes cuts like this.

tically a disk) to produce very fine lines. You might shape such a wheel for yourself eventually, once you are no longer a beginner. I don't recommend it for beginners. It takes too much time to produce and the disk wears down very rapidly. Most lines, even fairly fine ones, can be done with a standard mitre wheel. The usual tapered-point mitre wheel will therefore do for the general run of lines.

The mitre wheel, then, is your best bet for making straight lines and curved lines, fine lines and drags. It will do star shapes. They are perhaps the simplest beginning designs, though a measure of control of the glass must still be a part of the process. By pressing the glass to this wheel, then pulling it off and turning it 45 to 90 degrees and repeating the process, you can create a simple star shape. Achieving this by combining the cuts you get

from single pushes against the mitre wheel is usually the very first creation of a beginner on a mitre wheel. Try it. You'll be surprised and pleased at how easy it is. The design seems to come out of its own accord. These single wheel cuts can, by themselves, look like a football - very long and pointy. Combinations of such cuts may be augmented by manipulating the glass surface, maneuvering it to pick up desired quantities of the taper of the wheel.

Dragging the Cut

You can make leaves with the mitre wheel by "dragging" the cut. Learning to drag the cut is an essential hand motion. Dragging can be done with any wheel shape but, to my mind, most effectively with the mitre wheel.

Dragging provides a very dramatic end result by extending to the sides or "fading out" a standard cut such as a straight line, and thereby making it into another shape. Leaves, for instance, are done in this manner with the mitre wheel; this drag is a turn and twist hand motion. You will be pulling or dragging the glass upon the wheel. For a leaf, for example, you make a line fairly deep and, without taking the glass from the stone surface, move it with gradually decreasing pressure to the left side of that center line. Then place the glass back on the stone and move it to the right side of the line. Remember, you are always working on the bottom surface of the glass, pressing or pulling or, in this case, dragging it upon the turning wheel. With leaves, the center line becomes the central vein of the leaf and the drag to either side of it becomes the leaf shape. You should practice this. You must learn to control this drag so you don't provide too much or too little drag. Once you master the technique, you can knock out leaves one after the other. Use the mitre wheel as well to cut in the smaller veins to either side of the leaf.

Dragging may be best thought of as a controlled skid. You swerve first one way, then the other. It is one of the hardest things to practice in engraving, so don't get discouraged. The only way you will be able to control this particular skid is by acquiring "hand sense." Almost no one gets this technique right straight off. The drag cut involves the most hand motion of any cut and usually the most control. It's a matter of balancing out these two factors: motion and control.

The mitre wheel is, more than any other wheel, susceptible to wear. You use it for a time and then you must re-dress it. Obviously its prime characteristic - its point - is responsible for this extra wear and necessary care. None of the other three wheel shapes require the constant re-dressing of the mitre wheel since they are either straight out flat or have just a slightly rounded profile. Working eight hours a day with these wheels you would find you only need dress them every few months.

The mark made by a printy wheel.

The mitre wheel, however, used over the same time period, must be dressed just about daily.

The Printy Wheel

This wheel makes a "punt" cut, a punt being a circle. Its profile is much less rounded than the olive wheel, which makes more of an olive cut. You can combine such circles to make rosettes or chains or any variety of circular forms. While there is very little curvature to the profile of a printy wheel, what curvature there is, is important. If your circle starts looking more and more square, it's time to correct the wheel by re-dressing it.

Actually, the circle cut is quite a dramatic one in glass since it is so wonderfully symmetrical. Unfortunately, this situation can work against you when you are putting such circles together into a pattern because the slightest irregularity in spacing will stand out emphatically and give the work an amateurish look. It is precisely in maintaining absolute spacing between cuts (shapes) of the wheel that the beginner generally comes to grief. This is true whether you make chains or rosettes, the

usual run of shapes with punts. You will find you are either too close to the previous one or too far away. It can be extremely frustrating but you have to believe the touch will come. As I keep saying, it takes practice.

The Strap Wheel

This is the simplest wheel of all. It is a flat profiled, unmodified stock wheel right from the manufacturer. You don't have to shape it or do anything to it other than bush it for a tapered mandril. It will make many of the lines that a mitre wheel will make using the corners of the wheel, though I find strap wheels more awkward to use than mitre wheels.

The strap wheel is one you may initially do without since the mitre wheel will do pretty much everything the strap wheel will do. However, there are some applications (square objects for instance) where a strap wheel will make the shape better (more cleanly, more readily) than a mitre wheel because of its flat surface and sharp edges. However, the strap wheel is more for rough cutting than the finer lines you can impart to

Marks made with a strap wheel.

glass with the mitre wheel, which has many more uses. I suppose the difference between strap and mitre wheels would be the same as, in painting, a piece of charcoal might be used to rough out a sketch, but brushes must put in the detail. In this instance the strap wheel would (more or less) be the charcoal and the mitre wheel the brush placing the final and more detailed end result. For bordering edges, the surface of the strap wheel will make nice flat impressions that the mitre wheel can only do with difficulty.

Re-dressing Wheels

Learning to re-dress wheels is obviously a necessity since once a wheel wears, you are at a standstill until you can get it back into shape. You must, therefore, learn to adjust each wheel back to the shape you originally imposed on it. This technique is no different than when you first dressed the wheel except for two new problems: the wheel will be smaller due to wear, and it may have acquired irregularities from use that must be

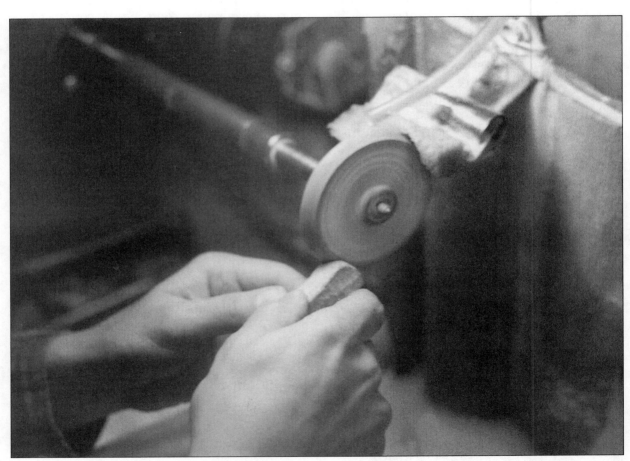

The mitre wheel in the photo is being re-dressed. The mitre has been worn down with use and must be re-shaped. This is done with a silicon carbide stick held by hand. Here the stick is being applied from below along the already existing near slope of the wheel.

The wheel on the left is being re-dressed to an olive shape by having the dressing stick applied at an angle of maybe 30 degrees. Such angles are pretty individual and depend on how extreme a modification you wish to make. The less of an angle you apply to the dressing stick, the more wheel edge will remain and the rounder the cut will be. As you angle the dressing stick more and more, the rounded edge becomes more and more tapered until you finally end up with a mitre wheel.

recognized and addressed. The actual re-dressing process, however, is the same as when you originally dressed the wheel: check for bounce and wobble and high points plus, now, possible chipping or gouging of the surface. There will be instances where a wheel may have been so badly used that re-dressing it might be more of a job than just replacing the wheel, though this is, frankly, not the norm.

At the same time, re-dressing can be tedious, more so perhaps, than dressing the wheel for the first time. For example, a mitre wheel doesn't necessarily wear evenly and re-dressing can be a question of which slope to bring back to the proper angle and how much time to spend doing it. Another factor, as mentioned above, is that as you use a wheel, it becomes smaller and thus more difficult to re-dress simply because of size. But small wheels are extremely useful for

certain purposes, so you don't want to just throw them out and start on a new one. Take the time to get these smaller wheels back into shape if you can. So, while re-dressing follows the basic dressing procedure, it can be more difficult because the wheels have now acquired imperfections to a greater or lesser degree from use.

Re-dressing is always time-consuming, especially when it has to be done on a wheel you like working with and want to duplicate. A lot of time can be spent trying to revitalize such a wheel and perhaps the time will be wasted, since the character of any wheel is literally shaped by the stresses of use, many of which can't be duplicated. It's quicker and easier sometimes to just re-dress to a standard shape than to try to re-create a specific shape that has been formed pretty much by individual hand pressure against the wheel over time.

Variations in Shapes

As I have said, variations of the four basic wheel shapes are totally within the needs and calculations of the individual artist. You can, for example, work out a specifically profiled wheel to do only letters. Or one to impose advanced mottling. You might want to take a mitre wheel and chisel or file out areas of the mitred surface to make a specific chipping effect. You are certainly free to experiment with such shapes, always keeping in mind that wheels do cost money and if you ruin one you will have to start over with a brand new wheel.

I like to use a wheel that is basically a mitre wheel except that the mitre has about a 1/4" flat surface in the center instead of a point. I dress my raw wheel to this profile. It is essentially a mitre without a point so it does not wear down as rapidly. The area from the top of this flattened point to the surface isn't important. What I have done, of course, is made myself a very narrow strap wheel. I find it easier to produce fine lines in this way by varying the pressure on the glass to left and right against the center edges. My mitre will last longer than taking the wheel to an actual point so I can get pretty much the same effect from it (fine lines) without having to be constantly re-dressing it. You can make wider or narrower modifications of this high strap wheel which is much easier to use than an actual strap wheel and has much more flexibilty of use.

As you can see, there's a lot of individual variation possible in wheel dressings. As you continue in this fascinating hobby you'll find many variations of your own that, eventually, may suit your hands and eyes better than the basic shapes. Once again, nothing is written in stone.

Chapter Six: Preparing the Glass - Scoring, Breaking, Grozzing, Cutting Shapes

Scoring Plate Glass

Scoring (cutting) and breaking out plate glass is done pretty much in the same manner as any other type of glass. It's not necessary to exert extra pressure because the glass is thick and you don't need a special surface upon which to cut. It is important that the under surface be smooth and free from glass chips. This is critical. Many individuals learn-

In cutting (scoring) plate glass, first draw a line down the glass for your cut to follow. Use a glass marking pen for a clear, bold line.

You can score glass with a "classic" cutter as shown...

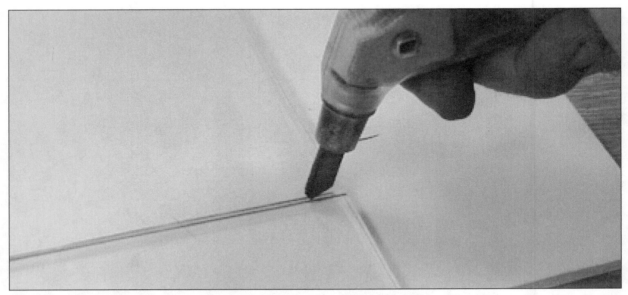

...or use one of the newer varieties of pistol grip cutters (shown). Either way, you can get a good score line. The "classic" cutter is usually employed by pulling it toward you holding it in the fingers of one hand. The pistol grip cutter, on the other hand, can allow the use of two hands (one on top of the other if you need additional strength) and is generally used by being pushed away from the user. For elderly workers and those of limited finger strength, the pistol grip cutter will serve the purpose well.

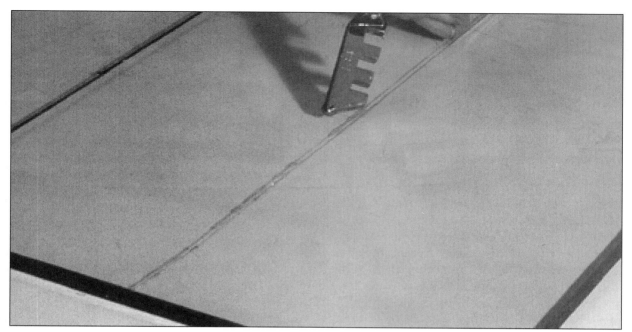

The score line.

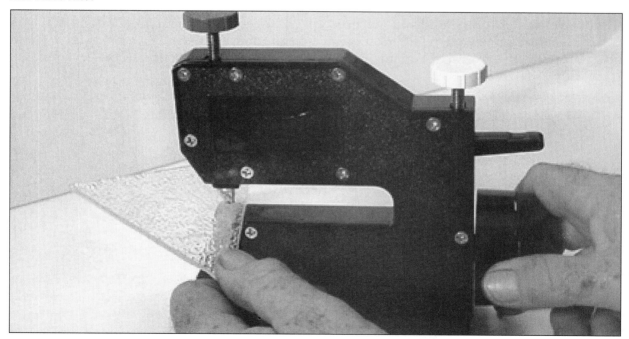

Another method of scoring glass (even on moderate plate) is the device pictured here called The Scoremaster. The glass is guided beneath the cutting wheel, which is then lowered onto its surface and moved along by turning the back wheel. You can score fairly large pieces of glass in this fashion if you hold them firmly.

ing to cut glass for the first time disregard this, either from anxiety to get on with the cutting process or from forgetfulness. Such glass chips will scratch or break your piece and may even cut you. Please do not brush such chips away with the back of your hand or any portion of your anatomy. Use a brush or a paper towel and brush them directly into the wastebasket.

Plate glass is not difficult to cut if you have the proper tools. You should have several cutters on hand that are specific for such glass. Most glass cutter manufacturers make cutters with wheels specifically suited to plate, and it is important that you use one of these rather than one that was made for some other glass. While you will probably be able to use another type, you will be making your job more difficult in the long run. It is just as easy to start doing things right in the beginning as it is to do them wrong and then have to undo mistakes.

For beveling (Chapter Eight) you will need two kinds of pliers as well as cutters: a plate glass breaking pliers and a running pliers specific for plate glass.

Cutting any kind of glass can be a scary procedure for many people and cutting plate glass doubly so. In point of fact it is a smooth, easy maneuver once you overcome your fear of being cut yourself. I have taught people from ages 14 to 70 to cut plate glass while on a ship crossing the Tasman Sea, a crossing that can be a lot scarier than cutting glass.

Pittsburgh Plate Glass makes fine heavy duty running pliers that are exceptional in their ease of running long score lines on heavy plate. As for breaking the glass along the score line, please don't try to use electrical pliers here. Rather than break the glass, they will more likely shatter it. If you use the proper tools all along you will save yourself a lot of time and effort.

When cutting glass it is necessary to follow these rules.

1. As stated, keep your workspace clear of glass "crumbs."

2. Keep your workspace tidy so that you have room to maneuver your glass without having to move other objects or crowding yourself.

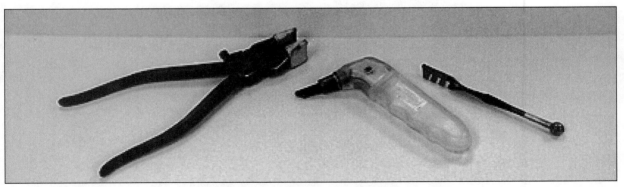

Glass cutting tools shown are left to right: running pliers (the jaws of which are applied to either side of a score line to "run" the score and thus break out the glass), and two types of glass cutters. Running pliers have a downward turned upper jaw and an upward turned lower jaw. The lower portion is placed beneath the score line, while the two downward points of the upper jaw fall to either side of the score line. This provides the fulcrum effect which applies pressure to "run" the score. Running pliers as shown will not work well on thick plate glass. A different type of device is used, to be shown shortly.

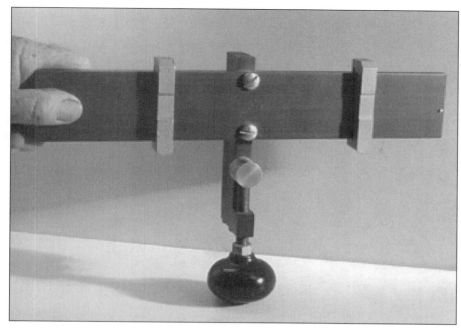

The plate glass breaker. This device uses a plunger on the bottom, which is worked by the black bottom handle to push against the score line from below while the two side pieces stabilize the glass to either side of the score line. As you turn the bottom handle, you increase the pressure against the score line from the bottom surface. Made by the Fletcher Co.

The plate glass breaker has provided enough pressure from below against the score line to start breaking out the glass. You can actually see the glass beginning to separate into two pieces.

Seen from the top, the view of the run is even more dramatic.

The two pieces of thick plate glass separated along the score line. This would have been rather a difficult operation without the plate glass breaker.

3. Don't wear sandals or any other type of open-toed shoes. Should a piece of glass fall off the table, it may fall on open toes and open them a little more.

4. Use a ruler or some other straight edge to score straight lines.

5. For circular lines, squiggles, or other types of freeform lines, make a pattern and either place this on top of your glass and cut directly to it, or place it beneath your glass and cut down to it. I find the first method preferable but I have seen workers using the second method and getting precise end results.

6. Since there are a number of different styles of glass cutters on the market, survey different ones and buy the one that best fits your hand.

7. It's best (most effective) to cut glass standing rather than sitting because you can employ the most force from your body. This does not mean you can't cut glass if you have to sit due to some bodily ailment. Individuals in wheelchairs can learn to cut quite effectively. It's just easier to learn standing.

8. Don't run your finger over a cut glass edge to see if it is smooth. More beginners have been cut this way than I can name.

Pushing or Pulling the Glass Cutter

In scoring plate glass, as in any type of glass for that matter, you may be an adherent of either the pushing or the pulling method. Some workers like to pull the cutter toward them; others push it away from them. Those that push the cutter say they prefer to see where they are going along the line of cut; those that pull claim they have better control of the cutter since they are not leaning out into space. Choose whichever method you are most comfortable with and that will allow you the best control of the cutting operation.

More important than which way you cut is whether you are using the proper cutter for the job. Interestingly enough, a dull cutter that plows a wide angle through the surface of the thick plate will provide a more effective break line for plate glass than will a sharp cutter with its thinner cut line. Cutters are available specifically for plate glass and you may want to save time, effort, and glass by acquiring one before starting work.

Breaking Out the Score Line

There are three standard methods for breaking out the score, that is for getting the glass shape you want out of the piece you have scored. It may sound like over-simplifying, but it is best to mention at this point that glass is not paper and you don't cut and break all the edges at once. What you do is cut and break each edge separately. Don't make all your score lines and then attempt to break out each one. The glass, so weakened, can break apart almost anywhere, ruining the piece and possibly cutting you.

The three standard methods are the tapping method, the use of glass and/or running pliers, and the fulcrum method. Let's look at the tapping method first.

Method 1: Tapping the Glass

In tapping plate glass, as opposed to "regular" glass, you can turn it upside down on the surface of the table and smack firmly over the score line with the ball of your cutter. This is quite the opposite of the method I advocate for tapping regular stained glass or single or double strength window glass where you hold the glass in your hand and tap from below. Plate glass is heavy to hold, the amount of force you would get from tapping from below would likely be ineffective, and the piece may slip from your hand. By placing the glass on the table, the force of your tap is increased because of the firm surface underneath.

The thicker the glass, the harder you must tap. With really thick plate, such as 3/8" or 1" you may not acquire enough force with the ball of the cutter. You may have to substitute a heavier implement, even a small planishing (jewelry) hammer (I did say "small").

The manner in which you tap also affects the score line. As the score begins to run (that is, deepen and start following the line of the cut), you should keep your tapping in front of this deepening line, which you will easily see penetrating the glass substance. If you don't do this, the running line may begin to deviate from the score line to a greater or lesser extent. A sharp tap in front of the run line may serve to bring it back where you want it to go and if you keep tapping in this manner you should be able to get a precise run right across the glass. Once this happens the two pieces of glass may fall nicely apart. If not, they will readily separate by hand.

Method 2: Breaking Glass with Running Pliers and Glass Pliers

There is a difference between breaking scored plate glass with glass pliers and breaking regular scored glass. The most efficient way to break out a piece of scored plate glass with glass pliers is to put the glass on the worktable and align the score line with the edge of the table. Grasp the excess glass with the pliers and pull. The pulling movement is mostly back and downward rather than the snapping motion that can be used with thinner glass. It's a good idea not to wear open-toed shoes during this procedure.

This method at first can be awe-inspiring for beginners, Because the glass is thick it appears at first unworkable. But you want thick glass

for engraving purposes. Oddly enough, plate glass is actually softer than most other types of glass and far less brittle than single strength glass. Yet 3/4" and 1" plate can seem a little threatening at first. To become experienced you will have to practice on alot of scrap glass.

Another type of pliers is the Pittsburgh Plate running pliers. Unfortunately the curves they break out can not be very acute ones. But for lazy long curves they will do fine. These pliers are used in the same manner as any running pliers. You line up the center of the jaws with the score line and press the handles together with a smoothly increasing force. The pliers are quite rugged and are meant to run scores on thick pieces of glass.

Method 3: The Fulcrum Method

To get proper leverage with this method I recommend using the handle of your glass cutter (obviously not a ball-handle). Depending on the thickness of the glass, you will need a certain amount of force to press down to either side of the score line that will now be raised off the table courtesy of the fulcrum. So, you see, there are all sorts of ways to score and break out plate glass and all you need to do is find which you prefer.

Grozzing

Grozzing is the act of removing extra shards and defects along the edges of the glass after it has been broken out; to more or less smooth these surfaces. The technique involves the use of grozzing pliers which are specifically made for the purpose. These pliers have sharp little teeth that can act as a file, sawing against the glass edge. You can also use grozzing pliers to nip off some of these unwanted projections. Although the advent of the glass grinder has pretty much allowed glass workers the option

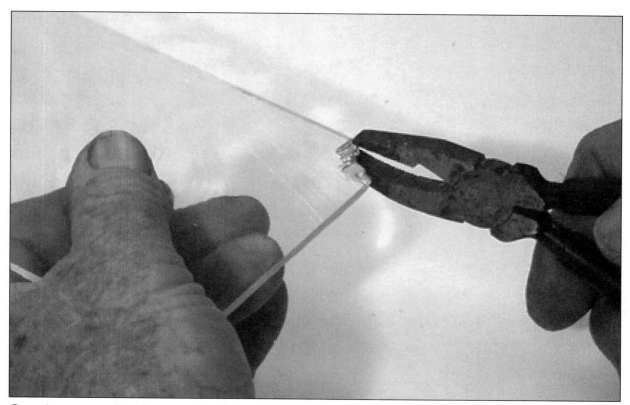

Grozzing means chipping away or biting away small pieces of glass that either mar a glass edge or that (as in the photo) are in the way of a design, in this case an inside curve at the corner of this piece. Grozzing is done with a grozzing pliers. This pliers has a rounded lower jaw and a straight upper one. The jaws meet at the edge of the pliers, which is where the force of grozzing is applied. Grozzing plate glass can be difficult because of its thickness. You should wear your safety glasses when grozzing any glass in case a chip of it flies off the pliers. When you grozz take small bites. The jaws of grozzing pliers are grooved so, in addition to their biting edge, they can act as files by running the inside of the jaws over a rough surface.

of using only this machine for the purpose, you should be familiar with grozzing pliers as an all-purpose hand tool.

The grozzing technique is pretty much the same for single or double strength window glass as well as plate though a stronger force may be required for plate both from your hands and your tools. If you are fortunate enough to own a glass saw, you can cut your pieces of plate glass to size with speed and dispatch. A glass saw, once a luxury, has now, for

many workers, become pretty much a necessity. There are several on the market; my preference runs to the Gemini Taurus II saw and the Diamond Tech International. The former uses a round blade and allows multi-directional cutting and is a joy to use; the latter uses a flat blade which (unlike earlier versions from other manufacturers) remains stable on the spoked wheels and provides a very accurate cut. Either of these machines will do a perfectly credible job for cutting a design out of plate glass.

The grozzed area of glass: the rough area is gone.

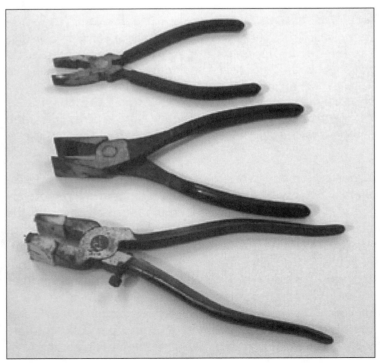

Three sets of pliers for working on glass. Top to bottom: grozzing pliers, breaking pliers (good for breaking out score lines of large pieces of glass. Note the large jaws), running pliers, the jaws taped to avoid scratching the glass when pressure is applied.

Points

If you are dealing with points in your glass pattern you must be especially careful, first in breaking out the piece to pattern and second when grozzing. When breaking out a pointed score line, pull with the pliers from the point itself rather than from any area surrounding it. This holds true especially when you are working with a long point. Pulling the score line at the point tends to preserve the "break out" arc; pulling from the middle of the score may well lose the point to an extent.

Inside and Outside Curves

These areas can be hand grozzed if you are using 1" plate, but if the glass is thicker, these areas may have to be broken out, by tapping. You may have to tap both from the underside of the glass (the usual way) below the score line, and then with the glass on the table tap directly over the score line. Such a maneuver allows the force of the tap to penetrate more readily through this thick glass. Another way to break out difficult scores such as these is to score both sides of the glass. Naturally you will want to be exact here so that the two score lines, top and bottom, will match. If they don't, the glass may break in a very irregular manner.

If you want curves, keep them gradual for an easier breakout. If your curves are too acute you will probably lose them unless you use a saw. Running pliers can be used on outside curves.

It is important that you don't try to save glass by squeezing the working area into a piece of glass that you can't really handle well. Make sure that you have enough excess glass on each side of the score line so that you can break out the score with the least amount of effort. Even the two pliers technique, that is grasping the scored area to either side with a pair of glass pliers and attempting to break out the glass in this manner, will not work if there is not enough excess glass for the pliers to grab onto.

Pattern Cutting on Plate Glass

There are a number of ways to cut a shape out of glass. My way is to use templates made of paper thick enough to allow a glass cutter wheel to run along their sides. I place such a template on top of the glass and use it as a cutting guide. However, other teachers prefer other ways, some of which involve placing the pattern or template below the glass, drawing the template on the glass with a marking pencil, using various types of machines to place the design. Whichever method you choose and make your own and are able to profit from in terms of comfort and production is the right way.

You can cut circles up to 4" in diameter with the device shown. Place the glass on the stand and press down on the spring-loaded shaft to lower the wheel against the glass. Then turn the handle and the circle will appear in the glass as a score line.

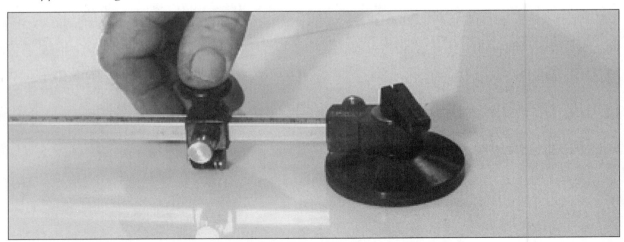

Another type of circle cutter uses a suction cup to center a long arm. The cutting wheel can be placed anywhere along this arm and screwed tight with a side screw. The thumb pushes the wheel against the glass and the arm takes the wheel in the proper direction.

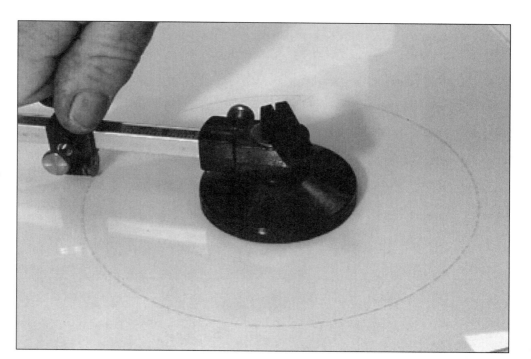

The scored circle.

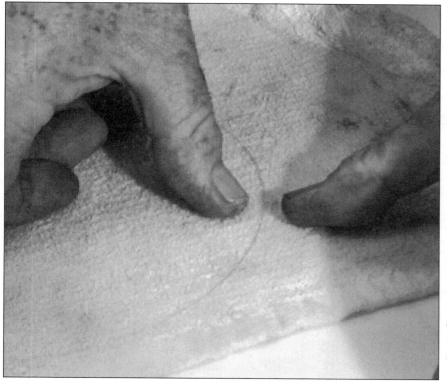

Breaking out the circle is done by turning the glass over onto a surface with some give to it, such as padded newspaper or a towel. If you use a towel, as shown here, make sure it is folded evenly with no lumps. Then press with your thumbs to either side of the score line all around the circle, not too hard but exert some pressure or you won't get anywhere. You will hear the glass start to ping as it separates. You may have to go around a couple of times to get the circle out, but you should be able to do this without cracking either the circle or the surrounding glass.

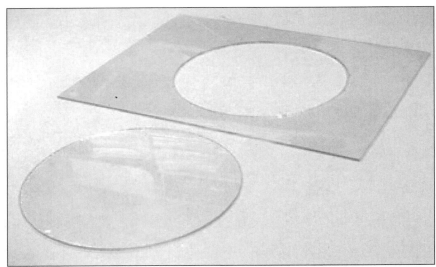

Here are the two pieces of glass: the circle and its background. You can use this technique with moderately thick plate glass or double strength window glass. However, to cut circles out of heavy plate glass you would be best to use a glass saw. Rather than purchase one of these expensive items for just a few shapes that you may want, try getting your local stained glass studio to cut the circle for you. Bevels already come in circles if engraving a circular bevel is your choice.

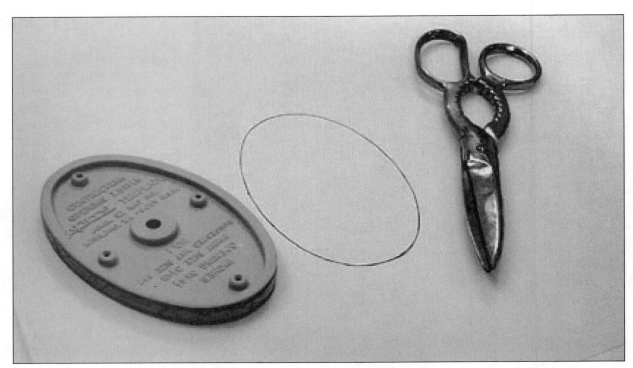

While there are machines that will cut ovals, it's far less expensive to cut one by hand. Start off with an oval template, available in art stores, a piece of heavy 80 pound white paper, and a scissors.

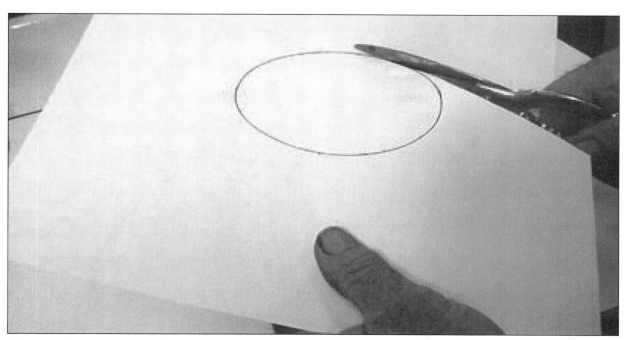

After tracing the pattern from the template onto the white paper, cut out the oval.

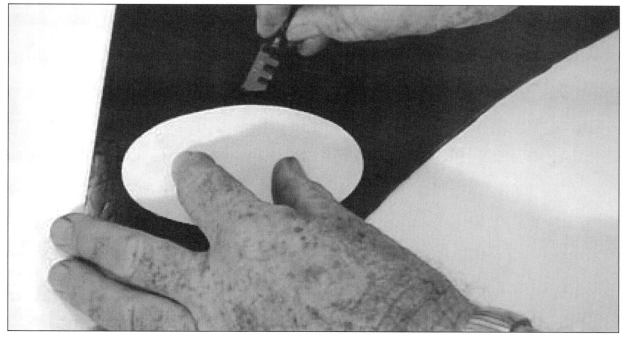

Place the paper template on a piece of flashed glass and, with the glass cutter, score around the pattern so the glass will match it. Score a portion at a time, don't attempt to score it all at once.

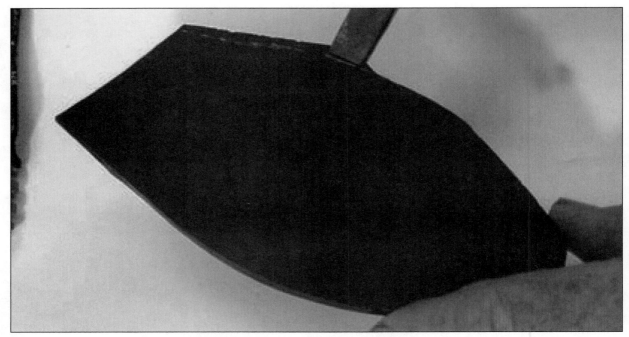

Use grozzing pliers to break away large pieces from the score line as well as small pieces of the edge.

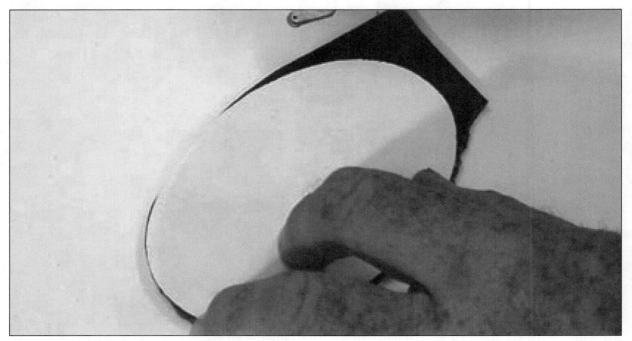

The glass is almost cut to size.

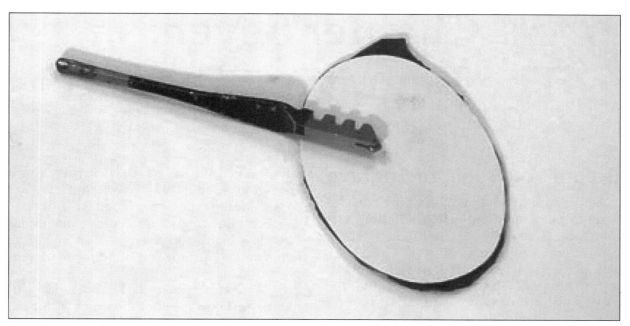

The glass now almost matches the pattern.

The glass and the pattern. The glass still has some rough edges but they can be smoothed with the strap wheel.

Chapter Seven:
The Engraving Process

Before You Begin to Engrave

Before you touch the glass to the wheel, I want to call your attention to difficulties you may face. Here are a few "peculiarities" you can run into right away.

1. Losing your glass. It sounds funny but it can happen. The machine can pull the glass right out of your hands if you aren't holding it firmly. Be sure to hold the glass with two hands and go against the wheel gingerly at first so the sudden pressure of the wheel against the glass doesn't toss it. Never hold the glass with just one hand. The torque of the wheel can easily pull a fast one.

2. Check the wheel now for bounce and wobble. Remember, you can't be too careful with these two gremlins, for they will show up in all your work hereafter if you don't catch them now. Refer to page 50 to correct these problems.

3. Start with a specific design. If you start trying to ad lib, you will end up with nothing more than an exercise in glass engraving, which is fine if all you are doing is practicing. But if you are looking to engrave seriously, you must start with a plan. Save "design as you go" for when you are more adept.

4. Check the rpms of the wheel. This usu-ally is noted on the motor. If it isn't, check with your supplier and make sure they are correct for the type of work you want to do.

5. For a first project, don't pick a mammoth size glass blank and attempt to carve all the floors of the Empire State Building. Start simple, start small.

6. Many first timers have problems with the water. There is either too much or too little. If too much, you will take your second shower for the day, spraying everything around you as well as yourself. Once more, the operative words are caution and experimentation. You don't want too much water and certainly not too little.

Putting the Glass to the Stone: Practice Exercises

As you start to practice with these exercises, not only your eyes and hands will tell you how well the engraving process is progressing, but your ears will too. A squeak or squeal from glass or wheel will tell you that something is definitely wrong. On the other hand, a nice whistle from the wheels means things are going well. And, of course, if you blunder badly, your own voice, raised in possible concern, will tell not only you but possibly the neighbors that you've gone off the track a little.

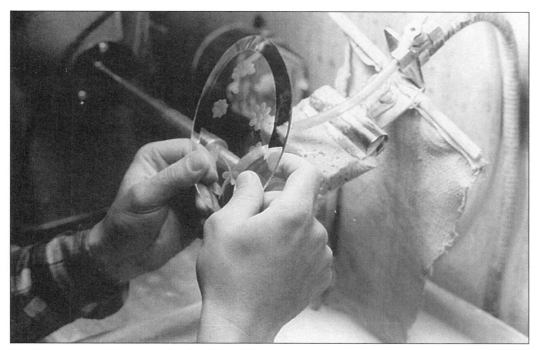

It takes two hands to steady the glass being engraved against the stone wheel. Glass is engraved on the surface away from the worker. For the initial cut, the glass is held upright against the stone wheel. Notice the position of the water hose and sponge.

As the work progresses, the glass may be tipped forward on the wheel to accomplish a design element. Note again that it takes two hands firmly holding the glass, not only against the wheel to allow for proper cutting, but to keep the glass from spinning out of control as the wheel turns against it.

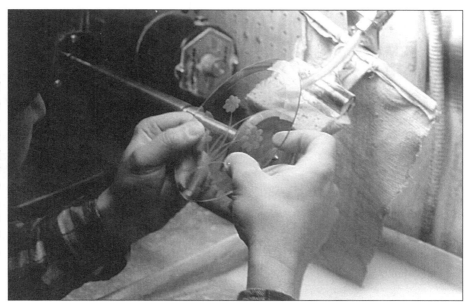

The glass may also be turned left or right to accomplish a design element. Here the worker has swiveled the glass as it is being worked, still holding it tightly to create a curved stem line for one of the flowers.

Practice deep cuts. Use a heavy piece of scrap plate glass for this exercise and practice making deep cuts in it. Hold the glass to the mitre wheel and exert pressure to allow the mitre to cut in. Calculate the amount of pressure such cuts require. You may have to re-regulate the water flow to allow for the additional heat of friction created. Make a number of these stars, practicing tipping the glass forward and backward to elongate the cuts. Try to make the cuts of equal length. Do your initials in glass in this fashion.

Practice with the mitre wheel. To the left is the leaf stem, to its right are the two sidewise motions of the hand (skids or drags) that make the leaf shape. Last on the right are the leaf veins put in with the mitre wheel in short touches against the glass. Practice all these motions one at a time, then put them together. Eventually, you should be able to do this in your sleep.

Practice with the printy and olive wheel. The central flower can have petals made by the olive or the printy wheel. Practice touching these wheels to the glass to produce such shapes as individual cuts, then try putting them together with the printy circle in the center and the olive petals, then reverse the process. The more you practice with what these wheels can do with simple shapes, the more hand sense you will develop. Make up your own designs using the three wheels. Also in this photo are more drag lines from straight lines with the mitre wheel. Make your straight line cuts, then tip the glass to either side to drag it away from that center line. Practice making two straight lines side-by-side and then dragging the cut from the bottom of each. You must learn how to maneuver the glass and only by constant practice can you do so. It's fun and you'll be very proud the first time you get it right.

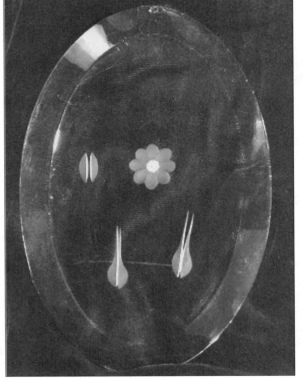

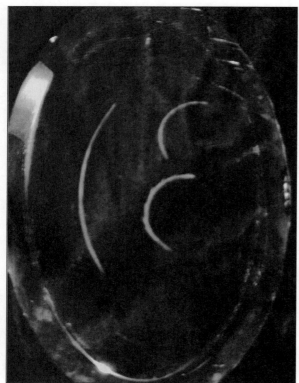

Practice curving lines. These are twist motions of the glass upon the wheel using the mitre wheel. As you may have guessed by now, the mitre wheel is the workhorse wheel. You should have had your fill of making straight lines and crosses with the mitre by now, so here's a chance to do something different. Start by making the less acute curved line on the left. This involves only a small amount of twist on the wheel. The more acute curved line in the upper right is done with a more angular twist. Hold the glass tightly enough so that it doesn't slip out of your hands, but not so tight that you lose all mobility. The curved line at the right bottom is really a collection of small curves, each building upon the prior curve. This is an extremely difficult exercise, but if you persevere you'll begin to develop your hand sense. You make the first slight curve, then build on that to make the next and so on until you get the effect of a curve with little spikes sticking out. Once you master this exercise you'll be right to feel proud of yourself.

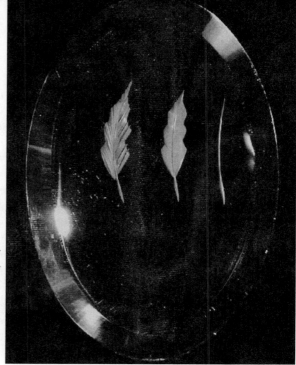

Practice a second leaf. A different leaf shape is provided here, but the basic process is the same. This shape is a little more complicated. You use the mitre wheel throughout, starting first with the stem. About a third of the way up the stem, place the glass and do a drag cut to the left and right to make the bottom portion of the leaf. Do the same to the next two thirds of the leaf, traveling upward and leaving the top half of the stem alone. Then apply the mitre wheel as in the left hand leaf to put in the vein lines. You can do this pretty much at random. Don't worry if some of the lines come out to a small degree beyond the drag portion of the leaf.

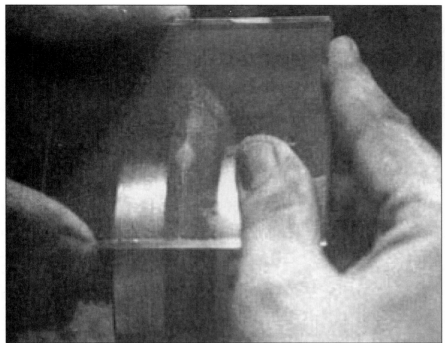

Practice with the water bubble. This is a classic view of the bubble of water that forms at the contact point of glass and stone and that serves as a guide to let you know that all is well. This bubble will not appear if there is not enough water (or will disappear if the water decreases to an amount below where it should be). If there is too much water, the bubble will widen to become more of a splash and start to spatter. Practice tipping the glass forward and backward and from side-to-side and watch how the bubble travels with you.

More practice with deep lines. See how the glass is turned after making the initial cross on the mitre wheel to make what will be the smaller inside crosses seen in the photo on the next page.

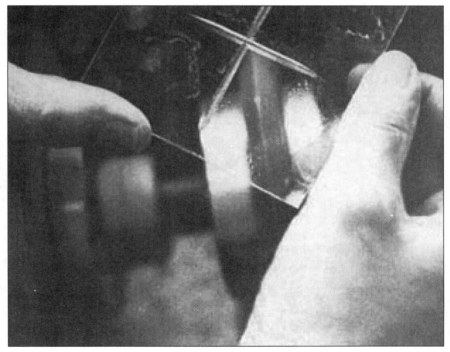

More practice with deep lines. The final resulting double cross begun in the photo on the previous page. Even a practice exercise like this can be made to look good. The right hand side rough cut border work was done with a strap wheel by holding that end of the glass flat against it and moving it with varying pressures.

Scrap glass practice. Practice making such crosses on scrap glass to get your hands used to turning the glass on the wheel. What's wrong with this one? All the lines are uneven in length. This means the glass was tipped too far forward or not enough backward. Not much control of the glass.

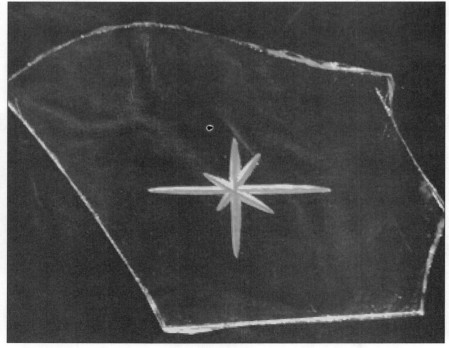

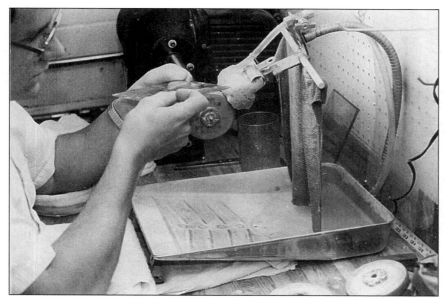

Moving the glass against the turning wheel. The glass piece is tipped to the left against a mitre wheel. The effect is to drag the cut line to the right.

The glass piece is held straight down against the wheel. The effect is to make a deep line.

The glass piece held horizontally. The effect would be an ordinary way to begin working on a design.

The glass piece is tipped forward. The effect would be to lengthen a line away from the worker.

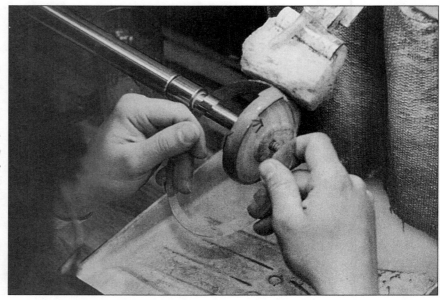

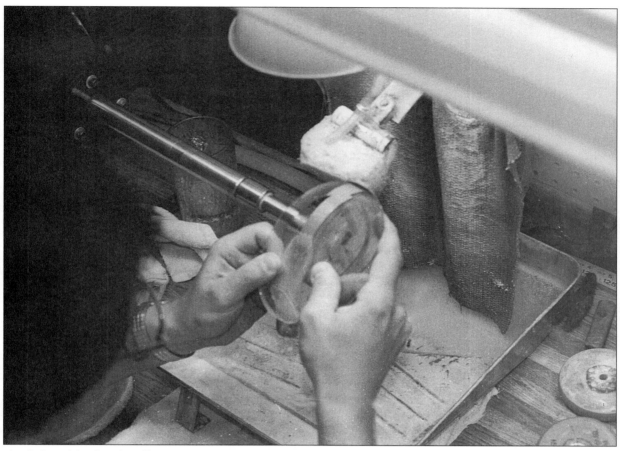

And tipped back. The effect would be to lengthen a line toward the worker.

Burning the Glass

If you don't have enough water flowing over the glass, you are liable to burn it. Burnt glass is no offering to anyone. Burning is actually terrible, terrible gouging of the glass surface. Once the glass has been burnt, the engraved channel becomes pitted and irregular. Burning occurs when there's insufficient lubricant (water) and the surface begins to heat up. This rise in surface temperature is the result of one the following:

1. The wheel is turning too fast. If you are pushing the rpms and/or trying to move the glass too fast against the wheel, it will burn. You are actually outdistancing its lubricant and presenting an unlubricated surface of glass to the stone.

2. There's not enough water on the surface. This usually occurs because of carelessness. Let's say you are working at slow speed and you assume you have sufficient water on and things seem to be going fairly well. It takes a while for the burn to occur at slow speed, and meanwhile you are concentrating on your work and being self-congratulatory and then, with no warning, the piece is ruined. All

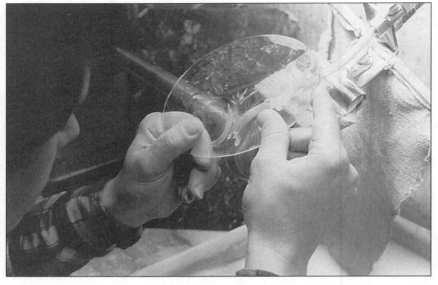

This series of photos shows burning from start to finish. Hopefully, this is the only way you'll know what burning looks like. Here, the engraving has begun with less water than is necessary. So far it doesn't look too bad.

because (usually) you are so eager to do the actual engraving, you take it for granted that the slow speed doesn't require a water check. Don't take anything for granted in engraving.

The look of a glass burn, even a small one, is unacceptable. There is only one look that is acceptable: a nice, satin finish. That's what your cut should have. Not a polished finish - you don't polish engraved work except for very special situations - but the cut should be devoid of any sort of scratching or line work. There shouldn't be secondary lines (which also occur from burning) running through the engraving channel. Minute burning shows up as inconsistencies in the channel or as white lines. Heavy burning is simply a mess.

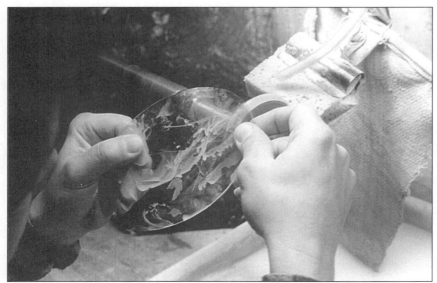

As the engraving proceeds with insufficient water, the milky haze starts to form on the glass.

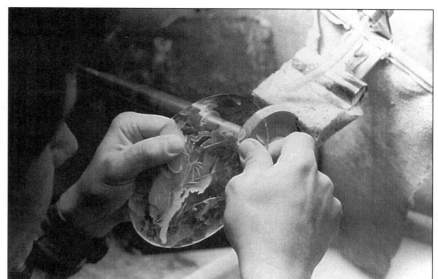

The milky precipitate gets larger.

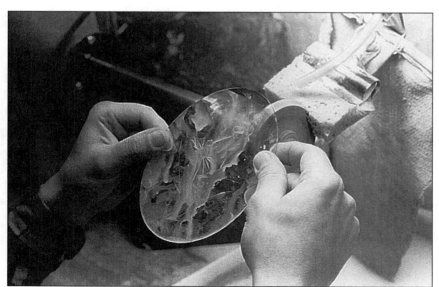

And larger still.

Milk White, Have a Fright

The first indication of not enough water coming over the glass is a milky-white solution that begins to cover the working area of the glass. This milky-white residue is the combination of the ground glass dust mixing with the small amount of water present and creating a sort of white paste. If you recognize this immediately, you can still save the piece. If, however, you keep going, irreversible burning will occur.

Of course, it is almost impossible (one would think) for someone to keep working with this milky precipitate all over the sight area. You can't see through it very well. For some reason, though, some beginners think this is the way engraving should be and just keep going. Be more alert than that.

Making a Design

You'll be surprised at how quickly you, as a beginner, can produce a design. It's so good for your morale to see a project actually come to life under your fingers after all the preparation and wheel corrections.

Choose a design and draw it several times on a piece of paper before drawing it on the

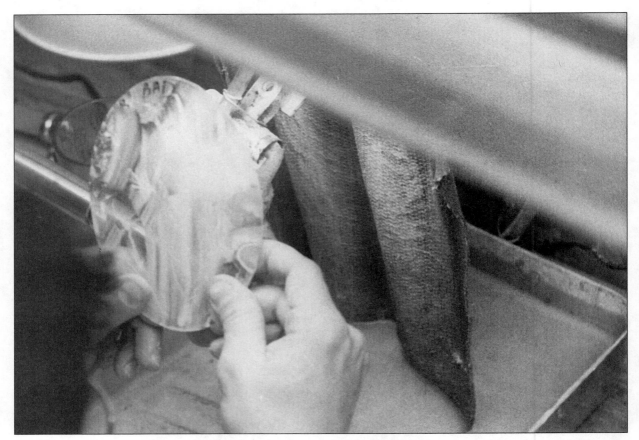

And here's what you end up with when burning has reached its final stage - a mess with a piece of glass totally ruined. And all because of lack of water.

glass. Remove any extraneous lines (in other words, simplify it). Especially as a beginner, keep the design as simple as possible. Complex designs can come later, when you're more adept. Drawing the design several times on paper will get your fingers and hand accustomed to the way the lines run. It's all geometrics, you see, lines and drag cuts for the shading, though the olive wheel will almost do the shading for you as you learn to work it correctly.

Draw the design on the back of the glass blank with waterproof ink. Don't bother to use waterproof markers. A fine-tipped marker, even though it provides a supposedly waterproof line, doesn't provide one that works well on glass. The marker line will come off unless you seal it with something and it tends to slide on the glass surface. If you insist on using a marker, use it on the front side of the glass, not the surface being engraved, so at least it will have a chance of remaining visible as you work. A grease pencil doesn't work well at all and even if it did, you can't get a thin line with one.

I use india ink with a pen or a toothpick to draw the design on the back of the glass blank and seal it with clear three-pound shellac. Spray or brush on the shellac after the ink dries. If done correctly, it will stay on during work. When you want to get the ink marks off, use a piece of fine grade steel wool or denatured alcohol. The shellac will come off as well. With india ink you can make the line as thick or as thin as you wish, thus closely following the original design. This is an advantage over a marker line. You can't change the quality of a marker line very readily, if at all. And if you're doing lettering, you know how important it is to change the line quality even within the same stroke. Using india ink, lettering can be done right on the glass, then sprayed with shellac. Once

the shellac dries, you can get right to work engraving precisely to pattern.

Some people think it's cheating to draw the pattern on the glass - that a real artist doesn't require guidelines, that an experienced worker should be able to control the material so well and so immediately that he or she can mentally transfer the design and work that way. Certainly there are workers who can do that, but I don't expect this of you as a beginner. As you progress in the art, you will be able to accomplish a lot of this type of transference. It's a matter of developing your perspective and knowing your material. This takes time. For now, draw your design on the glass and don't be ashamed of the process.

I want to emphasize another point about drawing the design. Even if you feel you are an accomplished craftsperson, if you hope to produce multiples of a design, I strongly suggest that, at least for the first dozen or so, you draw the same design on every single blank. This is especially important if the design is at all complex. If you do the engraving freehand, you will find the design elements starting to deteriorate as you go along, and by the time you compare design #50 to design #1, you might not be able to recognize it as the same design. In the ordinary course of events, design elements will shift to some extent. Despite the fact that you are using an engraving machine, the process is still considered a hand craft and material so produced can vary from one to the next. However, piece #30 shouldn't be a totally different design than piece #1. In most cases of mass-produced items, the customer buys only one of a series and will therefore have no means of comparison, but that's not always the case. If he is able to pick and choose from a collection of similar pieces, you don't want the procedure to get so far out of hand that your series gradually transposes itself into something totally different from the original intent.

Despite all this explanation, I have seen students spend bunches of time laying out their design on the glass, using all sorts of marking devices, only to see the design disappear before their eyes once they start engraving. With the india ink/shellac method you can readily design on the same side you will be cutting on (the side opposite you). This is the most precise way to follow a design and I recommend it, especially when you are working on thick glass. In such instances, looking through the glass with the design on the front and the cutting process taking place on the back is unsatisfactory because you must then look through the glass, through the design, and match it up to that spinning wheel. You'll never hit that line as precisely as you would need to do with a very complex design. You want the end result to be exact, every depth perfect, all points the same. You must draw everything out in such a project.

Things to Remember

1. You are working with glass, so you have to be careful how much pressure you apply when forcing the glass against the stone wheel. Too much pressure, especially in the case of a fairly large sheet of thin glass, can cause it to snap.

2. You can do various things with the same wheel, depending on your needs, so it isn't always necessary to change from one wheel to another. With an olive wheel, for instance, you can make the cut grow, even though the wheel is only 1/2" wide, because as the wheel digs into the glass, the oval cut grows up and down. With the printy wheel, the cut grows equally in all directions.

3. When engraving more complex shapes, you have to make the glass move in more direc-

tions. A simple straight line is made with the glass perpendicular to the wheel; a curved line is made with the glass half perpendicular and then twisted. As you start to turn this line, you make an angle. You can pull this angle and get still another effect. Practice angle turning and twisting. The way to learn engraving is to keep adding motions to ones you already know.

Making a twisting leaf is the most motion you can go through as consecutive flow - it involves turning, twisting, lifting, and angling the glass. That's a lot of facility. And you must do it all while maintaining the proper pressure against the wheel. If you lose this pressure in the midst of all this movement, you will slide or skid - both undesirable motions in this instance. Practice making straight lines, then start adding little curves to it. As soon as the glass starts to slide, pull back. You may be sliding because you aren't applying enough pressure against the wheel. Some beginners are very timid about pushing the glass to the wheel and don't allow the wheel any sort of purchase. That will allow the glass to slide. Of course, too much pressure will make too deep a cut.

4. Develop a feel for your material. Your arm muscles will respond to the wheel/glass combination and eventually will lock the glass in so it will not go anywhere. You don't want it to. This will allow you to make nice, constant motions with enough pressure to make good cuts. It's all practice and patience.

5. Develop perspective for the lines on the glass. This is a mitre wheel exercise. Start by making straight lines. You can make beautiful stars by just bisecting straight cuts. It isn't hard to make one straight cut, but it's somewhat more difficult to predetermine where the next cut should be to bisect or meet the first one. At what point do you start the cut so it will end properly? If cut #1 is just so long, then cut #2 has to be calculated against it. You can learn to compensate if that second cut seems to be

going astray; you must learn how to come up a little or down a little and start your second line with this in mind. Again, it's practice.

In actuality, you may get two different line cuts while trying to form one single one. Practice making connections between cuts - obviously cuts that match. Practice compensating when your second cut is started too close or too far away from the first one by tipping the glass up or down against the stone.

6. Positioning. It's important to position the line cuts right the first time so you don't have to spend time and effort correcting or compensating for bad cuts. Develop a spatial relationship so you can feel where the glass should meet the stone even before the cut begins. Compensating for mismatches only works where discrepancies are moderate, otherwise you can end up wasting a lot of time trying to make lines or shapes go together that have no such potential.

When you are doing line work, don't make a curve tighter than the circumference of the wheel. If you try to do this, your line will begin to chop, it won't look tight and clean. The smaller the wheel, the tighter the curved line you can make (one reason to maintain a supply of small wheels).

7. With any design, once it goes wrong there is a point of no return. You make a commitment every time you select a location for a cut but this location may be too far away from the grouping you want to meet up with, or it may be too close or it may be too up or too down. Once you find you have made a poor choice, it's generally easier to start over than to try to convince the glass the mistake is on its part. You'll never win that argument.

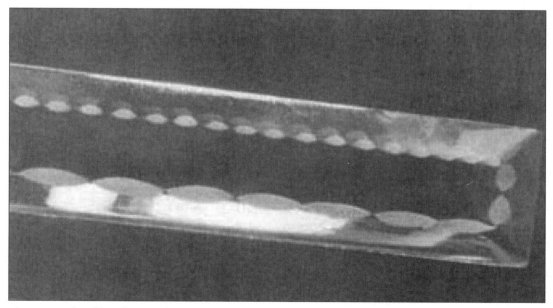

An example of border work on a piece of beveled glass. All you have to do is touch the beveled top edge to any of the wheels to get a particular effect. The small marks were done with a mitre wheel just touching the glass and moving very slightly. The larger marks were done with an olive wheel and were accomplished just by holding the wheel briefly against the glass edge. The marks on the short edge were done in the same manner with a printy wheel.

Deepening Lines (Depth Cutting)

In engraving you can go over the same cut twice. Or more. You can use a single cut from any of the wheels as the starting point of many cuts. This notion of re-passing - going over and over the same cut - is an important one. The quality of the channel, whether a mitre cut or an olive or a printy, changes each time you penetrate it. You must get precisely back into the same channel each time or you will have sloppy looking scratches around it. This alone takes practice. If you attempted to achieve any sort of depth in one pass, you would have to go so slowly to allow for that much glass removal that no human could do it. You would have too much wobble, not necessarily from the machine, but from your own hands. You would end up with a very unsteady looking design.

It's not much easier to do depth cutting in a number of passes but that is the way it must be done. Each time you add a little more pressure and increase the width of the channel. The idea is first to get your design cut out in its entirety, then keep rotating the piece and re-cut the channels you want to deepen.

Once you have the technique down, it's simply a matter of putting in the time. It becomes routine: rotate, deepen, cut; rotate, deepen, cut. And don't be tempted to push more in one area than another. Once you start pushing too hard you will begin to acquire inconsistencies that will really stand out. You want all cuts to be the same, so keep the speed of the wheel the same. You also have to find the pressure you like and stay with it.

That is not to say you have to make multiple passes every time you want to make a deep cut. You can make a small star, for instance, with the proper depth cut right away. But that's a small item. On a large piece of glass with a complicated design, you will definitely have to do some re-passing.

Incidentally, when doing any sort of complicated design, use thick plate glass. It's only a suggestion and some workers may disagree with me, but for my part, I hate to say how many times I tried a complicated subject with deep cuts on thinner window glass only to have it break more than half-way through.

Border Work

Border work is, by its nature, repetitive. That makes it subject to error, usually because the engraver gets careless or finds the work tedious. I happen to enjoy border work; it's a great challenge and wonderful exercise for the eye and hand. There's a certain restfulness about doing the same process over and over no matter what wheel you are using. Whether you are making dots or slices, because the process is repetitive, you must stay alert since one dot or dash misplaced can ruin the entire piece.

When doing repetitive border lines, first concentrate on cutting the individual lines out. Don't think about the depth of the lines yet. Not only will placing the lines allow you to maintain an even border and help with spacing, but it's too difficult to do everything at once and it's very hard to come in with any deep, deep cuts in a single pass. Really deep cuts take several passes - five or even more - to get the proper width and depth. You do understand, of course, that as you deepen a cut, because of the nature of the stone wheel, you also widen the cut.

What If Your Masterpiece Breaks?

If the glass breaks as you're working on it, there are several alternatives:

1. Throw up your hands and scream.

2. Destroy your engraving machine and become a hermit.

3. Try selling the broken pieces as anthropologic discoveries.

4. Start over, considering the reason for the breakage and figuring out how to avoid it next time. After all, if you were able to achieve the work to the point where it broke, you can redo it correctly. All you are out is time.

While you should always take your work seriously, you should never consider it as literally engraved in stone. Glass breaks. That's part of its character. But the idea of the work and the impetus behind it can never be destroyed. Don't get so fixated on one piece that you feel its loss would be detrimental to the history of mankind. Maybe it was one of a kind, but you can do it again. You may do even better next time. Practice makes perfect after all. You may have lost a little money, you may have lost a little time, but you can do it again. Only the glass is fragile. You are tough.

Chapter Eight: Beveling

Introduction

Those of you who want to purchase your bevels ready-made and concentrate only on engraving may still want to pay attention to this chapter, which will touch on some of the basics of the beveling procedure. The reason for including this information is that as you progress in your engraving and your skills and ambitions grow, you may start looking for bevels more fitting to individual pieces. It's unlikely that you will find commercial bevels of various thicknesses and tones; of different reflective and refractive qualities; of odd densities and impurities (as in old glass); and in a variety of shapes and sizes. While these qualities may provide intrinsic comments on the engraved surfaces and can immeasurably increase the artistic quality of the final design, they are not necessarily available over the counter.

In such cases, the only way to acquire individual bevels of varied shapes, thicknesses, angles and other characteristics is to make them yourself.

Beveling your own products is a very satisfying endeavor. True, it requires more time and a beveling machine, but such machines are now available for the tabletop and are not pricey. Beveling your own final products can result in end results so striking, so creative, and so satisfying that the time spent learning this ancillary procedure can end up making it on a par with stone wheel engraving since

the two go together almost hand in hand. Accordingly, this chapter will take up this procedure in some detail to give you an idea of what the beveling experience is all about.

A Brief History

The history of beveling is somewhat vague. The craft appears to be more or less a direct descendent of glass grinding. This technique reached its apogee in the cut crystal marketplace. Actually the notion of putting a tapered, polished edge on a piece of glass - which is what beveling is, taken down to its basic formula - did not develop from any artistic urge but rather developed for a technical purpose. English manufacturers of scientific instruments as far back as the early 1800s used glass where they could because it was easy to keep clean. They found that grinding glass stoppers and bottle necks not only provided a tight fit, but allowed for hermetic air sealing within the bottle. The stopper wouldn't fall out even when the jar was inverted. Ground glass stoppers were used in pipettes as well, where small amounts of liquid were to flow. These turnable stoppers allowed for easy motion but prevented any extra drops from getting through except where the hole was drilled.

The English and the French still argue today over which country discovered beveled glass. It is the least important of their arguments, but there is a certain comfort in knowing that it is important enough to remain a controversy.

Taking things a step or so further, beveling eventually became a decorative device. In fact, it was decorative long before it became "artistic." We turn to the old time English manufacturers of scientific instruments. A number of their instruments can be found in museums, crude electronic ancestors of things we take for granted today. Holes were ground in glass to hold the various components which were neatly placed inside. Of course, glass offered a small coefficient of expansion aside from being easily kept clean and it allowed you to see what was going on inside as well. But in addition to their practicality, such instruments were designed to be pleasing to the eye. Often the beveled glass plate of the instrument was a fairly thick glass for sturdiness, and this made it easier to encase it in a bezel so that it could be attached to something. This in turn made it easier to use.

In the United States glass beveling became popular in the early 1900s and most of this beveled glass was turned out in Chicago.

Categorized Operation

If you were to visit an old industrial glass beveling factory, you would see production divided into strict categories. The glass grinding, for instance, would be a department of its own. This one section in its two or three aisles might encompass more than 250 square feet with grinding stations on either side of each aisle. These machines would be belt driven, since this was long before the use of electric motors. That doesn't mean such machines weren't efficient. They were (and still are where they are used) very efficient.

At each machine would sit a man whose only function was to grind off the excess glass from each "blank" or template to give the bevel its initial shape. Today we call this "roughing" the bevel. Every so often men would come down the aisles with large push-cart stands and pick up the rough pieces of glass and distribute new blanks. The roughed pieces would be taken to the next aisle of 50 or 60 operators who would do the next step in the process - smoothing the glass. And from there the glass was taken to the polishers in still another aisle.

Workers didn't know how to do other men's jobs. This was not to keep the overall process secret, but rather for efficiency's sake. It would have been counterproductive to have one person do each and every step.

The Henry Lange machine still lives on, at least in the workshop of Calvin Sloan of Star Bevel Studio in Riverview, Florida. Sloan rescued this machine from a field where it was on its side with a tree growing through it. Back in his studio, minus the tree, and after many tender ministrations (such as soaking the wheel, shaft, and bearings in oil for a month) and some rebuilding, the machine works like a charm.

A Henry Lange smoothing wheel. Note the towel draped over the edge of the machine to catch and absorb the water that is flowing onto the wheel. The spotlight is correctly positioned to shine on the work area of the stone to reflect through the angle of the glass to check how the smoothing is progressing.

Bird in Tree engraved on blue flashed glass by Jan Matuszak, Studio One Art Glass, Milwaukee, Wisconsin.

Beveled and engraved treasure box by Jan Matuszak, Studio One Art Glass.

Rectangle clock with bull's eye fractured streamer with wheat stems and grasses by Jan Matuszak, Studio One Art Glass.

Glue chip border with floral engraving on an octagon clock by Jan Matuszak, Studio One Art Glass.

*Rectangle clock with
engraved daisies
by Jan Matuszak,
Studio One Art Glass.*

*Wheel engraved oak
framed clock
by Jan Matuszak,
Studio One Art Glass.*

Oval and diamond candle lanterns by Jan Matuszak, Studio One Art Glass.

Desk set by Jan Matuszak, Studio One Art Glass.

*Treasure boxes and candle
lanturn by Jan Matuszak,
Studio One Art Glass.*

*Engraved ornaments by Jan Matuszak,
Studio One Art Glass.*

Wood-framed decorative panel with an engraved hummingbird and flower by Jan Matuszak, Studio One Art Glass.

Flower with decorative bevel and starburst rondel by Jan Matuszak, Studio One Art Glass.

Engraved swan ornament by Jan Matuszak, Studio One Art Glass.

Knotwork panel with center brilliant work circle surrounded by small circle bevels by Calvin Sloan, Star Bevel, Riverside, Florida. This shows how pencil bevels can flow in a line around a center piece and keep the eye moving around the panel.

Victorian style decorative panel using champagne and clear colored plate and pencil bevels showing inside and outside curves and glue-chipped highlights by Calvin Sloan, Star Bevel.

Three starburst panels with faceted, glue-chipped and engraved bevels with various textured glass by Calvin Sloan, Star Bevel.

After the bevels had been semi-polished (on a cork wheel) and then polished (on a felt wheel with cerium oxide), they went to still another area for assembly and crating.

Overall production here furnished beveled glass windows in multitudes. Every day scores of them were shipped all over the country. These were not just bland, factory-made reproductions, but were highly individual. Many were lovely and intricacy was the order of the day.

The major glass machinery manufacturer for beveling was the Henry Lange Co. in Chicago. Before the company began to produce these units, a number of beveling plants had their own machines made specifically for them. Such individual machines built to individual specifications could be expensive.

The Henry Lange Co. was the only major manufacturer of glass machinery from 1890 to about 1930 when, with the advent of the Depression, glass beveling went into a decline. Within the next ten years, public interest in stained glass windows came to the fore, since beveled glass was not considered to be anything special. Bevels were assembled into a cheaper form of art-glass windows than stained glass. Many factories preferred to make stained glass windows rather than beveled glass ones to avoid the additional expense of a beveling machine. The economics of producing the two types of windows were probably about the same as they are today, that is, the value of stained glass and beveled glass was equal to the value of the labor involved.

The Henry Lange cast-iron machines were extremely large and heavy. Each beveling station was a separate entity and each weighed about 650 pounds. Four stations were necessary in the beveling procedure. Initially, as I said, these machines were belt driven, but as time went on, many were converted to electricity. They were never driven by foot power because the grinding, smoothing, and polishing wheels were too massive to be worked by a treadle. The original power was delivered by way of a line shaft suspended from the ceiling of the factory. Every 10 feet or so there would be a bearing assembly. A belt, either driven by a small steam engine or, in Chicago, by a municipal steam engine, was placed at the end of the shaft. This type of device could furnish a number of factories with power. If you were located in the industrial district and you paid your taxes, you would share an alleyway with other factories. Here would be a large source of steam power and you simply tapped into it.

Imagine those old days in one of those factories. Listen to those old leather belts, 4" or 5" wide, a joy to hear. Listen carefully and you can hear throughout the shop the leather belts ringing, the big flywheel turning, the slap, slap, slap of the leather belts, the turning of the wheels, the continuous slapping of those leather belts…

Beveling Terminology

Beveling terminology is fairly specific, but it can be confusing since different people mean different things by the same terms. In most instances, the confusion lies with the term bevel itself. I use the word bevel for the entire piece of glass, the edges of which have been slanted at less than a 95 degree angle with the existing surface or as in "pencil bevels" with the remaining surface edge nonexistent. I also use the term for the particular slanted edge itself, so far as its length is concerned.

I use the term mitre for the width of the bevel. If you hold a beveled piece of glass directly in front of you, the bevel runs from left to right whereas the mitre runs up and down, the bevel being the line and the mitre being the slant. The angle is the line made by the mitre with the untouched glass surface. It is also the line between contiguous bevels. The mitre controls the angle. Thus the bevel is the mitre plus the angles, in short, the entire piece of glass.

If you understand these three terms you will have little difficulty following this chapter or talking with another beveler. The following terms in the beveler's vocabulary are also essential.

Roughing wheel or station: The first wheel that is used to get the glass shape. It may be a cast-iron, steel, or diamond wheel.

Smoothing wheel: The second wheel used in beveling. It can be "a natural wheel" such as a Newscastle sandstone, or an artificial one such as an aluminum oxide or cast iron.

Cork wheel: The third wheel used in beveling. A solid cork wheel is used with pumice for polishing.

Fiber wheel: The polishing wheel in a vertical machine.

Vertical machine: A machine in which the wheels are aligned vertically rather than flat as in a horizontal machine. The advantage of a vertical machine is that it takes up less space; the disadvantage is in the small amount of wheel surface offered.

Felt wheel: The final wheel used with jeweler's rouge or cerium oxide to give the perfect finish to the bevel.

Scalloping (or actually "gouging"): An effect that results from allowing the glass to remain too long in one spot on the roughing wheel or on the smoothing stone.

Tapering: Where a bevel starts at one width and ends at another, diminishing in some instances to a fine line.

Step bevel: The process of beveling within a bevel, giving the effect of steps going down to the edge. This is also called step mitreing, since the secondary bevel is within the mitre, but both terms are used.

Cross bevel: Where a bevel changes direction within its plane, that is it angles in a slightly different direction from the beginning of the bevel to the other side.

Notched bevel: A bevel in which the angle has been worked with an engraving wheel to make discreet scallops along the edge. The scallops can be spaced or contiguous, giving a beaded effect.

Diminishing bevel: Instead of running the length of the glass edge, the bevel fades into the surface part way across. It is a planned process of not completing the line of the beveled edge.

Horizontal wheels: Wheels that lie flat, the worker uses the wide surface.

Slurry: This is a mix of grit and water that flows onto the first (roughing) wheel to help remove glass fairly rapidly.

General Principles of Glass Beveling

Usually a beginner will start with straight line beveling and go on to inside curves, outside curves, and S curves. These are the four basic beveling shapes. Doing outside curves, which include circles and ovals, is the more difficult procedure. The S curve demonstrates a pencil-bevel end result, that is, one in which the entire surface of the glass becomes beveled. There is no flat surface on an S-shape pencil bevel, so there is no place where such a bevel might be engraved. Such pencil bevels are used, therefore, in the engraving process, as border pieces surrounding the inner engraved circle or oval bevel.

Other techniques that can be imparted into the beveling technique aside from engraving include what are referred to as "brilliant" work and working with mirror. Working with mirror opens up an entirely new galaxy of effects using the same techniques that apply to clear glass. All of these effects can be combined with any type of beveled piece. For instance, often pencil bevels are notched (actually an engraving technique). This process started in the Victorian era, the golden age of beveling. Such a process is called brilliant work because it enhances the reflectability, hence the brilliance, of the glass by increasing the number of facets on its surface. Engraving from this standpoint can thus also be considered brilliant work.

Stock up on various thicknesses of glass. Don't rely on the same type or thickness of your plate; such glass varies greatly in its makeup, especially glass that is years old. A lot of plate glass can be readily obtained from your local glazier - he just throws it away. Old glass, especially, will give you some startlingly differed bevels both in reflectability and in the prism effects that are the main functions of beveled glass edges.

Four Basic Steps

There are four basic steps in the beveling process, although I occasionally use five if I am using all vertical wheels. These steps are divided into the different wheels or stations that are employed: roughing, smoothing, semi-polishing and polishing.

Each step has its own problems and delights. Most of the problems involve trying to correct a defect that was either in the glass to begin with, or one that was imparted to it by the worker. In either case, such defects are correctable but only to a point. That point is reached once you have removed so much glass that you no longer have the room to make the correction. I have seen individuals struggle for a much longer time than the piece warranted to make a correction only to end up throwing the piece away because distortion had entered the picture. Another major problem, and perhaps the most frustrating one, is "faceting" or "waves" that appear within the surface of the bevel. These are caused by uneven smoothing on the second step, the smoothing stone.

S Shapes

Of all beveling shapes, the S shape is the most difficult for most people to cut. A hint may be helpful. After scoring, turn the blank upside down on the worktable and tap over the score. Start your tapping on the inside curve of the S because that's where you will lose it (mostly) if you are going to lose it. Tap slightly in front of where the score runs so that the line won't have the tendency to run its own way. On the ends of the score, where the glass is weakest, support the glass with your hand. These end cuts can be very deceptive. By the time you have the whole shape almost out, things can still go wrong and the piece may break. It takes a lot of practice to make S shapes for beveling.

Safety and Cleanup

Beveling is a messy operation, so wear work clothes, use an apron, and don't set up your machine in the kitchen or living room. You must have a source of water; if you are working in a garage, you can use a garden hose. Use a drip bucket to catch excess water as it flows out of the machine. Dump the water outside; don't put it down the drain of your sink because the grit that is in the water will clog it. Don't put this excess water on your plants because the compounds of the beveling process may kill them. Keep children away from the beveling machine and all beveling apparatus.

Fingernails can be a disappearing factor since there is really no way to protect them. Don't try wearing gloves because they will rip. Skin is safe enough, although if you insist on working with tiny pieces of glass hour after hour you may get some abrasions. Certainly you will bevel your nails.

It's a good idea to clean your beveling machine each time you use it. Sadly, many professional bevelers don't bother to do this until the buildup of debris becomes an obstacle to their work.

Strike a Position

When beveling, choose a position that is most comfortable to you. You can sit or stand depending on how you best relate to the machine if it is a floor model. There are plenty of tabletop beveling machines on the market but, again, you can choose the best beveling position for yourself even with such machines. Beveling, with any type of machine, is a slow process. You must learn as you go, getting a feel for the procedure as you progress, just as in engraving. There is no single way to hold the glass against the beveling wheels; indeed, you may prefer a different stance against particular wheels.

Light

As you bevel, learn to look at your glass from time to time in different kinds of light. Natural light is best, but you should also hold it up to artificial light. This helps you to detect flaws, especially facets. One kind of light will show a flaw that another kind will not. Move the glass around as you look through it. Facets may show up only when the piece is being moved and the light plays on them. If you haven't polished your bevel properly, reflected light may show this up the best, whereas under direct light it may look perfect. This can be a bit disconcerting.

The Beveling Procedure

Reduced to basics, beveling is a process where the edges of a piece of glass are angled from some point on the surface to the rim. The process requires a special machine with special wheels that abrade the glass to a lesser and lesser extent, thereby making the surface smoother and smoother. There are generally four wheels - roughing, smoothing, semi-polishing, and polishing - though some bevelers add additional wheels for special effects. These wheels can be individualized or combined into a single machine as is the present practice with contemporary machines. The operator holds the glass by hand to each wheel to obtain the maximum effect from it.

The roughing wheel is critical to acquire the actual cut of the bevel; from there on each wheel makes the angle of the glass that you want to acquire smoother and smoother. It's not a difficult procedure but attention must be paid to keeping that angle to each wheel in exactly the same manner or "facets" will occur.

Facets

Facets are actually miniature bevels within the bevel itself that occur from not maintaining a constant angle against the wheels of the beveling machine. They will be more or less visible to the naked eye but they will break up the light coming through the bevel in an irregular fashion so the prismatic effect is distorted. Facets are not what you want to see in your completed bevel, they are imperfections that can be rather difficult to get rid of once they occur. How do you get rid of them? You can keep trying to polish them out, but sometimes the more you polish the worse the facets get and the more frustrated you get. Often, where facets are very noticeable you may have to discard that piece of glass and start again, literally from scratch.

The Prism Effect

The beveled edge affects light rays in several ways. It accentuates refraction of light waves which tend to travel in straight lines. When these strike the surface of the glass angle (bevel), they are reflected in a scattered pattern. The eye sees this as glisten and sparkle, almost like fire being elicited from the glass. Light waves hitting the beveled edge just right may also bend, breaking up into their constituent colors. Thus a prism effect is produced, an actual coloration of the glass edges comes into play. This can throw a wash of color onto the floor or walls of the room, depending on where the glass is placed. The effect, to say the least, is striking on its own; with an engraved centerpiece it makes the engraving stand out much more than it would on an unbeveled piece of glass. Which, of course, is one reason why so much glass engraving is done on bevels.

While beveling in the past was looked on as a decorative rather than a fine art, today craftsmen combining it with glass engraving find it a powerful tool for their imagination.

As usual, the glass does most of the work in providing dramatic flair so even the novice can produce surprising works of art. From this aspect alone, the craft is immediately rewarding. As technique is refined with further use and experimentation, beveling becomes another essential modality in the armament of the craftsperson who works in glass as a total artistic expression.

Beveling Machines

Beveling machines all operate in much the same manner, though some have greatly improved wheels over others and while some are floor models, others are designed for the tabletop. You may be able to use your beveling machine (check with the manufacturer) for materials other than glass, for instance to polish metal or stones or any material that will be amenable to the speed of the wheels. In general beveling machines are quite adaptable and it is fun to wander out of the realm of glass from time to time and poke your nose into other modalities.

Beveling wheels can be all vertical or all horizontal or a mixture of both; the ease of working with one type or the other being strictly individual preference. The wheels are usually four in number (the various stations) and use various substances. Roughing wheels may be com-

The Studio Model Beveling Machine from Denver Glass Machinery.

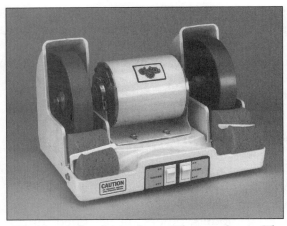

A tabletop machine from Glastar Corp. The wheels shown are for roughing. The wheel on the left is a 100 grit wheel and the right is 600 grit for smoothing the rough surface left by the 100 grit wheel. Notice the sponges in the tray, which are filled not only with water but a special coolant

The MMB-16 from Denver Glass Machinery. This is basically a beveler that has been divided into two seperate units - a roughing/smoothing station and a polishing/brilliant cut station.

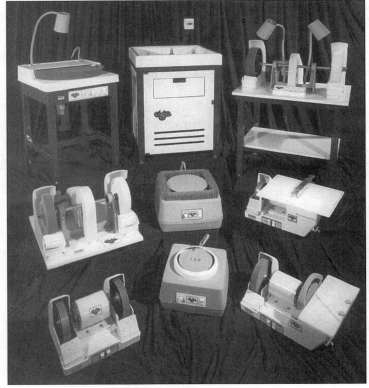

Glastar Corp.'s family of beveling equipment. Specializing in hand-crafted and shape bevel machines. Glastar offers many options: disc and wheel, bench-top and stand-alone stations, all made with the best motors to powerfully give you the vibration-free speeds you need to grind, pre-polish and polish.

posed of steel or cast iron or special stones or even diamond wheels may be used here. Polishing wheels can be felt, cork, fiber, or impregnated fiber. Speed is the requisite here, speed versus expense. A horizontal wheel gives faster service than a vertical one since there is more surface traveling under the glass edge at one time than with a vertical wheel. Tabletop models take up less space than do the large floor models and are best where space is limited. Your purchase of a machine may also depend on the sizes of bevels you want to produce. Most bevels don't exceed 12" in overall size.

Some substances are used in conjunction with the various wheels to improve performance, such as pumice and cerium oxide with the polishing wheels. Grit (silicon carbide 80-100 grit) may be used with stone wheels. The stuff tends to fly off the wheels as they turn so you would be wise to erect some sort of shield arrangement to maintain cleanliness. Many machines come with a fence plate around the top surface to keep spraying to a minimum. You can acquire a number of different wheels for the various purposes and change them at will.

The machines are meant to do two things to the glass: to roughly shape the bevel, that is to grind away excess glass until the proper angle is achieved, and to then smooth that angle which has been so ground. When glass is ground it becomes opaque, sandy, and will not transmit or reflect light well. Therefore, the surface that has been ground must be rejuvenated to its former clarity. The initial process is called "roughing," the second is termed "polishing." There are various stages within the polishing procedure where different wheels and their adjunctive agents are used to acquire the final "fine" polishing which is the aim of every true beveler.

Beveling machines come in various sizes and shapes, from large standup cabinets to smaller tabletop machines. How much room you intend to devote to this craft will, of course, determine the size of machine you get. The Denver Glass Co. has various sizes of machines to fit any ambition and pocket book. The Glastar Corp. is also a reputable and dependable manufacturer of beveling machines. Both these companies sell new machines. As for used machines, I do not recommend that you purchase a used machine unless you have had it checked out by an expert. Otherwise you will have no way of knowing if the wheels are running true, or if the thing will break down shortly.

Most contemporary machines are actually three or four machines in one, each unit being a separate but contiguous entity. That's a great space saver. Or you can acquire a roughing station or a polishing station alone, as was pretty much the situation in the past. These single purpose units may serve well in commercial enterprises where a great deal of work is being mass-produced, but they are barely acceptable in hobby studios. Here some type of machine that combines all the necessary units would serve the purpose best. Such would be the Denver Glass Studio Model Beveler together with the Denver Glass I V 16. Both of these machines are workhorses. I also recommend the Glastar line of beveling machines, many of which are unique tabletop models that will give excellent service practically forever.

Beveling Plate Glass

One of the joys of beveling is transforming otherwise useless material such as broken pieces of plate glass into unique objects of beauty. Various types and sizes of plate glass abound, much of it on the way to the scrap heap, and a lot of that old glass is glass with character built into it. You can pick up scrap glass from your local glazier or from salvage yards. Plate glass comes in various thick-

Two ways to store wheels both for beveling and engraving. Hang them on the wall, providing you have that kind of wall space, or store them in a trough under or on a table. Courtesy of Star Bevel.

This window shows curvatures of pencil bevels in the center, which is an engraved piece of circular glass.

nesses, from 3/16" (most stock bevels are this thick) on up.

The design and style of a bevel depends as much on the thickness of the plate as on the cut. And the thicker the glass, the deeper you can make your engraved portion as well as the steeper you can make your bevel. Most automatic machines such as the massive line bevelers use 3/16" plate and make what is called a "skin" bevel. This has a fairly thick edge, since only a minimum of glass is removed from the surface. There isn't that much of a prism effect here; another reason why you might want to do your own bevels. To get a good prism effect the glass would have to be additionally ground by the machine, which would mean additional wear on the heads and the manufacturers, who sell such bevels fairly cheap, might prefer to

Close-up of beveled ovals in combination with a piece of glue chip glass that is mounted within a square that is also a bevel.

Close-up of inside/outside curved bevels surrounding a centerpiece of three glue chipped bevels. The sinuosity is very appealing. Courtesy of Star Bevel.

defer this procedure or up their prices.

You don't have to worry about wearing out the wheels on your beveling machine. My advice is to use a really thick piece of plate glass to get as dramatic effect as possible from the beveled edges. The steeper the angle of the bevel, the more of a prism effect you will get. Thickness of plate can go from 1/4" to 3/8" and some artists work in glass up to 1" thick to get the effects they are after. You won't get this kind of thickness in store-bought bevels. All sorts of engraving techniques can be employed on thick glass.

Old plate glass of a greenish tint may be found, which will give a warm sheen to the bevels because of the excess iron content. New plate, on the other hand, provides a colder, bluish sheen. Engraving on either one will give a different dramatic effect.

Beveling Stained Glass

Stained glass can also come in various thicknesses, especially the so-called "antique" or "mouth-blown" glass. Usually flashed glass (glass of two colors, one color laid over the other) is used. Flashed stained glass, either beveled or plain, may also be used in engraving, where the top color is ground away to show the second color to illuminate the engraved area. As far as beveling (or engraving) is concerned, since most stained glass is about 1/4" thick, you can't get a very deep bevel or, for that matter, a deep engraved surface.

Towels and Buckets

Beveling, like engraving, can be a messy affair; the polishing aspect is especially so since the material is placed on the wheel and tends to fly about. New types of wheels have the polishing ingredients imbedded in them and this cuts down considerably on the amount of cleanup necessary. It's a good idea to wear some sort of apron, even over your work clothes. Towels are useful and paper towels doubly so. A dip bucket or rinse bucket is a useful item to have, and you should have a different one for each wheel. (I discuss the different wheels, or stations, later.)

Separate buckets will help to avoid contamination from one wheel to the next by carrying

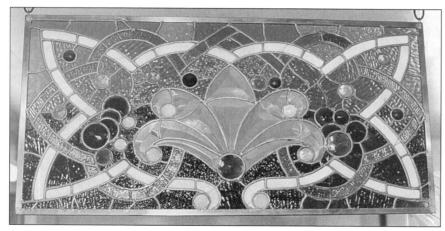

A window showing a central flower design of bevels in combination with stained glass and glass jewels. Courtesy of Star Bevel.

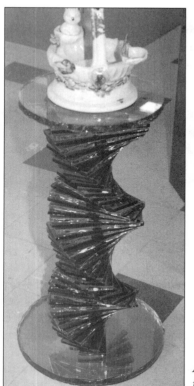

Close-up of varying beveled shapes in discrete clusters yet tied together in the overall design. Courtesy of Star Bevel.

A cluster of beveled squares glued together with ultraviolet setting glue to form a table base. Courtesy of Star Bevel.

up dirty water onto the glass. Contaminating your wheels can spell ruin as far as good beveling is concerned. It is also a good idea to have the various wash buckets alongside you, rather than sitting on the floor. This will obviate the necessity to keep bending over whenever you rinse. The more comfortable you are, the more time you can spend beveling. The same idea, of course, is also true of engraving.

Every time you change wheels, make sure you wash the glass well. It doesn't matter so much if you transfer from a fine grit to a coarser one, that is, go from cerium oxide to pumice. But it does make a great deal of difference if you transfer from coarse grit to a wheel that uses a finer one, as in going from the roughing to the smoothing wheel. Obviously in such an instance you want to wash away all the coarse grit before transferring to any polishing wheel.

Silicon Carbide, Pumice, and Cerium Oxide

Silicon carbide, pumice, and cerium oxide are abrasives that are applied to the glass surface with the various beveling wheels. Of the four (usual) wheels, only two are used without any abrasives added: the smoothing wheel and the fiber wheel. Silicon carbide is the coarsest abrasive used in beveling. Anywhere from 80 to 120 grit can be put onto the cast-iron roughing wheel (the wheel you start with). Grit becomes finer as the number goes up: 80 is a coarser grit, for instance, than 100; 100 is coarser than 120. You have to reach a compromise with yourself as to how coarse a grit you want to start with. The coarser the grit, the more rapidly it will abrade the glass, leaving a rough surface that you then must smooth. If you begin with a grit that is too coarse you will spend a lot of time on the smoothing wheel getting rid of a scarred and pitted surface.

The second wheel, or smoothing stone, uses no applied abrasive, as previously mentioned. The only abrasive is the wheel itself. The grit number of the smoothing wheel is 300 to 360; obviously much finer than the 80 to 120 of the silicon carbide used on the roughing wheel.

Pumice is a finer abrasive than silicon carbide, not necessarily in particle size, but in hardness. Actually a type of volcanic glass, it is used for fine abrading. Dentists may use pumice to clean teeth. Pumice comes in grades from extra fine to extra coarse. I suggest the use of a medium-to-coarse grit to aid in removal of facets from your glass that were not properly removed on the smoothing stone. The cork wheel, the third to be used, has a grit number of about 600.

The last wheel, the felt polishing wheel, uses the abrasive cerium oxide, a fine powder. I use it at a grit of 1,000, which is very fine indeed. Many old time bevelers used jeweler's rouge on the felt wheel. This is an iron oxide powder that works well as a polishing agent, but it is messy to use and stains everything it touches, as well as the skin.

You can see that the grit used in beveling gets finer and finer as each process leads to the next, and glass removal gets slower and slower with each process. Beveling requires patience more than almost any other aspect of working with glass.

You might ask the question: Why use all these different materials? Why not just use silicon carbide for the entire process, merely substituting finer and finer grits? Well, you can. The old time bevelers had three cast-iron wheels and a single felt wheel. They ran the glass down in just this fashion, substituting finer and finer grits of silicon carbide on each cast-iron wheel. It's a faster method than I have described and even produces a more accurate bevel. The problem is the weight of these old machines makes them difficult to move around and the cast-iron wheels are awkward and require heavy supports and bases. Practicality of cost and space lies in favor of the first method, especially for hobbyists, but even for most commercial enterprises.

Selecting Glass to Bevel

Before choosing a piece of plate glass for beveling, consider the following:

* Is it the proper thickness for what you want to do? Don't worry if it looks as though it is too thick to cut. Don't compromise your design for this reason alone.

* Does it have scratches that will show up in the bevel? An old piece of glass that has been through the mill may have such defects. Look carefully.

* Is the glass old or new? Old glass is greenish or yellowish on its edges; new glass is bluish.

* Be sure the glass you choose will allow your pattern to fit its surface with plenty of overlap. It is a mistake to try to save glass by squeezing your pattern into it. Cutting a difficult shape should have plenty of glass all around.

* Hold the glass up to the light to make sure it doesn't have any hidden flaws. Some plate glass hides cracks or chips within its width. As you begin to score such a piece, the pressure you apply can cause these flaws to crack the glass.

A word more about scratches. Don't have the notion that a scratch in the glass you intend to bevel can be polished away during the beveling procedure without having any effect on the glass itself. The polishing wheels are not big erasers. It is true that you can polish out very superficial scratches to an extent on the felt wheel, but if you have a scratch in the glass that you can feel with your fingernail, forget it. To remove such a scratch you will have to take away so much

glass from that area to get below the defect that you will end up with a distorted surface. In some cases this distortion will be a worse defect than the scratch and after all that polishing you will still have to discard the piece.

* Make sure your glass is absolutely clean. If it has a haze, get it off; if you can't, discard that piece. It's frustrating to get a fine cut and start to bevel and then notice that the surface haze is alive and well and intends to live with you.

* Check the glass for any sharp points or edges and remove these before starting to cut. Because of its thickness, plate glass can break unevenly, leaving small shards sticking out of the cut line. Remove such shards by sanding with a piece of wet carborundum paper.

Do you have to start off with a perfectly cut piece of glass before starting to bevel? The answer is no. Some craftspersons who carry over stained glass techniques into working with plate glass automatically assume that the piece of plate glass must be finely grozzed (that is all surfaces precisely taken down to pattern) before the next step, beveling, can be accomplished. While this is the case in stained glass technique, when working with plate, especially thick plate, grozzing to this extent can lead to fractures. So grozz (smooth out) the more obvious defects in the surface, but don't overdo it. The first of the beveling wheels, the roughing wheel, is a terrific grozzer. It will take off those points and sharp edges with ease and with much less risk of fracturing the glass.

Flawed Surfaces

If you select a piece of glass that is chipped on one side, it doesn't matter if the glass chips further on this side as you work it. You will be beveling this flawed side, so the chipped area will be ground away. Naturally you must be on guard to avoid any chipping to the final piece. Any chip that shows in the finished bevel spells ruin. If you do have the misfortune to chip out a piece of surface during the beveling procedure, don't waste time and effort trying to disguise it by further grinding. Just throw the piece away and start again.

Hint: When pattern cutting plate glass, turn your patterns upside down against the worst of the two surfaces. This is the surface that you will then grozz or tap against as you maneuver the piece into shape. The surface that is flawed is the surface to be beveled. You might want to keep this in mind by actually marking such a surface with a glass marking pencil. The letters BTS (bevel this side) will stand out and speak for themselves. This may sound like overindulgence but when you are working on a number of glass shapes, beveling, cutting, engraving, etc., it is all too easy to pick up an unmarked piece and, in the heat of the moment, start grinding the wrong side. All it takes is that first pass through the machine to ruin what might be a difficult piece to cut, and then you have to recut the piece and waste time and effort and increase the frustration index.

Water

Beveling and engraving are techniques that use a lot of water and if water is not handled correctly, it can lead to a mess. Your hands will probably be wet most of the time. You will have to keep wiping water off your glass as it is being beveled or engraved in order to see what you are doing. If you wear glasses or are wearing protective glasses, you will have to wipe them off from time to time.

Flaws and Frustrations

Facets

I've mentioned this before but since this is possibly the most frustrating of the flaws, it is worth going over it in some depth. These waves within the area of the bevel are mostly caused by the smoothing stone, the second step in the beveling process, and they are mostly removed by the smoothing stone as well. They can be difficult to remove and many workers will try to remove the more obvious ones only and let the rest go since the process of removal is so long and tedious. Unfortunately, facets break up the even flow of light through the bevel and are disconcerting to the eye. They should be removed to whatever extent is possible and reasonable. If you use the smoothing stone correctly you should get very few of these waves

Sand

This is not really sand; it's the microscopic pitting that may be left within the bevel from the grit used for roughing, the initial step in the process. However, it looks like sand in the glass and so it is called that for want of a better name. All of this "sand" or "texture" must be removed in succeeding steps, right down to the very last pit. You will, of course, rinse off the glass piece after roughing so the surface grit will be washed away. What remains of this texture within the glass may be removed in the second step, the smoothing wheel. If you still have "sand" in the bevel after this step it means that you either have not worked long enough at the smoothing stone or you are not working at this wheel in a proper manner. Alas, it is the smoothing stone that also makes facets, so you may be adding these, quite unaware, while concentrating on getting rid of the sand. That's fun.

Scratches

Keep in mind that each step in the beveling process, each wheel removes traces of the previous wheel. Obviously, you are removing glass at the same time. But there should be a balance between the amount of glass you can remove and the amount of surface that remains flawed by scratches or any other problem. Especially scratches. Removing sand pretty much is taken care of by the wheels in their natural process of acting against the glass. Scratches are a different matter. You may see none when you pick up your glass initially (obviously you don't want to) but when you look at it again in a highly reflective light, you may. Scratches are often caused by the smoothing stone if this stone is being run too dry or it has become contaminated with the silicon carbide from the previous roughing stone. Mainly it's a question of having enough water running onto the stone and constantly rinsing off the piece of glass you are working with. Keep the dip bucket handy.

Cloudy Bevel

A bevel that is not polished sufficiently (on either the third or fourth stations, the semi-polishing or the polishing stations) will look cloudy when held up to the light. A finished bevel should be sparklingly clear. If your bevel is cloudy, you must go back and repolish. The fault lies somewhere in this process. Either you have used the wrong polishing material, the wrong wheel, the wrong speed, or you have not given enough time to the procedure. A cloudy bevel is a common mistake and one that points a finger at your technique.

Uneven Bevels

Here the mitred edges (the bevels themselves) are uneven in width. This is discon-certing and will occur if you don't check your bevel constantly, especially during the roughing process (the first wheel). Attempts to re-straighten an uneven bevel can be quite tiresome. If you attempt to straighten it out in one swoop, it is all too easy to overcompensate and end up with the line going the other way. You have to go very slowly and keep checking the width and make sure the ridge is evening out. Often it is better not to waste the time trying to fix this problem but simply to start over.

Mismatched Mitre Angles

Mitre angles should go directly into the corners of the glass. When they don't, you end up with only a partial bevel and your work will appear amateurish and sloppy. The mitred angles can be thrown off as the first occurrence in a number of steps in the beveling process. The problem is compounded when you fail to keep checking the width of the bevel from the top line to the edge of the glass, that is the measurement of the mitred portion. Use your ruler and check constantly. If you keep a check on the glass edge, you can automatically check the angle of the mitre. The edge of the glass will tell you all you need to know. If the edge is thinner in one place than in another, you know you have to remove more glass to make the surface even. When you do this, the angle (mitre) has to come out right to the corners of the glass.

Bowing of the Mitre

This is also a smoothing stone problem. It is mainly the result of either too much pressure on one part of the glass against the stone, or uneven pressure, or the glass was left too long in one area of the stone while the stone was turning. Usually the mitre tends to bow in the center because some workers (for some reason) seem to concentrate more on the ends of the bevel, assuming that these are the areas where they will have trouble or because they feel they can work more comfortably in the center later on. This defect is readily correctable; all you need do is concentrate on smoothing that center section - once you notice that it is off.

Ready-made Bevels Vs. Hand Bevels

As I said at the beginning of this chapter, there are good reasons for wanting to make your own bevels for engraving. You may think that machines make better bevels than can be made by hand. Actually machines, in the main, do make pretty good bevels, but they can also come up with some whoppers, especially where straight mitres are concerned. This is because the machine heads must be constantly adjusted to maintain perfection. And the truth is that, more often than not, such constant tinkering with the machine provides more downtime than some bevel manufacturers can afford. So inferior bevels are sometimes passed over by manufacturers. The logic seems to be that the inferior bevels will appear to have been produced by hand because of their very defects.

Which brings us to the "Perfect Bevel." There really is no such thing. It's an ideal that seems to be forever beyond those who work in the craft. Theoretically, the perfect bevel would be as clear and undistorted as the entire surface of the untouched glass. This is almost a contradiction in terms, since the first thing you do in beveling is deface that piece of glass, then try to make it perfectly natural once again.

Beveling involves defacing original material, just as engraving does; both are terminal processes. The best that any beveler or engraver can hope for is to get back as close as possible to the purity of the original surface.

Questions and Answers About Beveling

Q: Couldn't a guide or jig be set up to help me hold my glass at the correct angle against the wheels of the beveling machine?

A: After a few hours of practice you will find that a jig is useless. Your eye is the best guide. A jig has to be pre-set for each different size bevel. This takes precious time, and it also can just get in your way. Bevelers for years have trained their hands and eyes to develop a "feel" for holding the glass against the wheels; in the end this is the only way.

Q: Does it matter in which direction the beveling wheels turn?

A: This depends on your preference. Most beveling machines have the wheels turning away from the worker. Because beveling can be a messy operation, you might find the wheels turning away from you will help make it less so. Also, with the wheels turning away, there is less drag on your arms. If you prefer to have the wheels turning toward you, you have to reverse the polarity of the motor by changing the wires running from the motor to the shaft.

Q: What type of lighting is best for beveling?

A: Natural lighting is always best. However, an overhead fluorescent will work fine.

Q: How can I help speed up my work?

A: The best way I know is the mass production process - that is, do all the roughing first, then the smoothing and so on. Also knowing what to expect from each wheel and training your eye to quickly spot defects will certainly help.

Q: How long will the wheels last?

A: With proper care and use you should get hundreds of hours from your wheels.

Q: How often should I clean my machine?

A: There are no set rules but I advise cleaning after each use. Your spray heads could become corroded and not function at their best. Or a problem could arise if too much glass ash and cerium oxide accumulates in the pan. This could clog your drain.

Q: Can I reuse the cerium oxide that is in the bottom pan of the machine?

A: I wouldn't. Cerium oxide is a very fine polishing powder and anything that contaminates it could reduce its efficiency. The white powder in the pan of the machine is glass ash. If this gets into the cerium oxide mixture, it could scratch your bevel. Also if you have used pumice on your cork wheel, the pumice residue would also contaminate the cerium oxide.

Q: How much water should I have spraying on the wheels?

A: The spray heads in the Denver Glass machines are designed to spray as wide as the wheel. If the force of water is too great, the mist from the faucet will be wider than your wheel; hence it will spin off the nut or flange and give you a bath. On the other hand, if the spray is not strong enough, only part of your wheel will be wet. That's not good either.

Q: How often will the wheels need to be dressed?

A: A hard question to answer. If a very light touch is used continuously on the diamond wheel, it will need to be dressed fairly often since this kind of touch will tend to distress the wheel more than a heavy touch. The softer wheels, the fiber and the felt, also need to be dressed often depending on how much use they are given. Every time a wheel is dressed, its size is reduced (just like engraving wheels). Such smaller wheels can be used on smaller bevels.

Glass Against the Roughing Wheel

The roughing wheel is somewhat of a misnomer since the wheel by itself doesn't really do the job. The roughing is done by a combination of the surface of the wheel (either cast iron or stone) plus the grit that will be flowing onto it in the form of "slurry." Grit is usually 80 grit (the more coarse) or 120 (finer). If you have two roughing stones, as some bev-

This studio has two roughing wheels, each of which uses different grades of grit. The worker will start with 80 grit on the first wheel as shown. The grit, as slurry, is falling onto the turning wheel for the reservoir on the slide. Courtesy of Star Bevel.

On the second roughing wheel, the worker has 120 grit, a much finer grit, to begin smoothing out the bevel. Courtesy of Star Bevel.

elers prefer, you would first apply the glass to the rougher grit and then go to the second stone with the finer grit.

The slurry is grit mixed with water. You control the water so that a heavy mud (the consistency of molasses) is produced. This slurry flows down onto the surface of the wheel from a slide or pouring spout that is part of the machine mounted above the wheel. You want neither too much nor too little water in the mix. If there's too much water, the slurry will spray all around and you'll slurry the walls. If there's not enough, it won't rough the glass properly; in fact it may scar the glass. The slurry should be of a consistency that will flow between the wheel surface and the glass and, as the wheel spins, can be thrown to the sides of the machine where (hopefully) it is retained by a railing for the purpose. Slurry can be used over and over. It's best to gather it up with some sort of trowel, however, not your hands, since the mass may contain sharp pieces of glass.

Once you have your slurry to the proper consistency coming down on the rotating

wheel you are, yourself, ready to roll. The first thing to do is to even up the glass blank to match the pattern you have chosen and grozz the rough edges down.

After you have done this you are ready to rough the sides. If you are roughing a straight line, the technique is simply to hold the glass against the wheel firmly and run it back and forth as the wheel turns.

The technique for roughing an outside curve is different. Here you will not be traveling back and forth across the wheel to any extent, though you may want to move the glass slightly. Instead of going back and forth you will be imparting an arcing motion to the glass. This, plus the shape of the piece, may make it more difficult to get comfortable with the glass in your hand than with the square piece of glass. Beginners tend to make their outside curves too slight along the mitres, or, in other words, too thick on the edge. I find that there are several ways to comfortably rough this curve depending on the size of the glass. With fairly large pieces of glass, where it will obviously be extremely awkward to do the entire curve at one time, do small sections at a time holding the glass at a fairly steep angle. Try not to cover more surface edge than you can handle, imparting this arcing or rolling motion to feed the next section onto the wheel. You can control the glass more effectively this way than by holding it still; the motion also helps to prevent facets from forming between the areas being worked on.

Another way is to arc the entire curve at one time, forming it as a complete section. Here the glass must be small enough for you to be able to control it. Both ways will work well once you get used to them. I hold the glass at slightly less than a right angle to the wheel. If I am doing a long edge I must be careful that the portion of glass toward the rim doesn't grind faster than that portion toward the center where there is less grinding surface. Always keep in mind that the outside portion of the wheel is spinning faster than the inner surface. Use this to advantage and try to keep your glass at this area to speed up the process.

Maintaining the Angle of Outside Curves

As you work the outside curve across the wheel, try to hold the same angle all around. It is better to start out with a half inch angle rather than timidly going for a quarter inch one and assuming you can always make it wider. It is more difficult to widen the angle than to get it measured up properly to begin with. If necessary mark the width of the angle with a ruler and a marking pencil and use the line as a guide. If you keep the edge steady and check it from time to time you will be able to keep the mitre in line.

With an outside curve, as with a circle, you work from glass edge to beveled edge. You can't match up sides as with a square because there are no sides to match up. At least with the outside curve there are certain relationships: for instance the two mitred angles at the top and the one at the point (the slightly unground border between the two arcs).

Outside curves are the most difficult (I feel) shapes to mitre because you really have nothing to go by. It's beveling by the seat of your pants. I start my outside curves by selecting one half of the glass (an arc) and beveling it all at one shot. I rough the entire edge of that arc with a smooth rolling motion, holding the glass diagonally across

The rough grozzed edge of the glass can be sharp to handle. The first step is to smooth the edge flat for safe handling. This is quickly done on a wet sanding belt. The result is a square flat edge that will make it easier to grip while grinding.

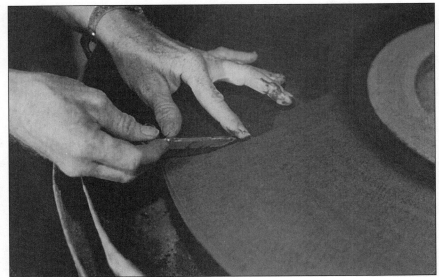

Holding the raw glass firmly against the cast-iron wheel that is covered with slurry, the worker begins the beveling process. Note that the glass is against the outside surface of the wheel, since that portion is spinning faster than the inner portion.

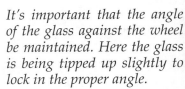

It's important that the angle of the glass against the wheel be maintained. Here the glass is being tipped up slightly to lock in the proper angle.

the outer margin of the wheel. This motion is repeated two or three times. Looking at the bevel shows me that it is getting slightly wider toward the point (that portion closest to the rim of the wheel, which is the border between the glass edge and the bevel). I twist slightly to the left, opposite to the way I am standing, and replace the glass on the wheel.

Now the point is facing the center of the wheel. In a short time the mitre has evened off. This process is repeated until the width of the mitre has been reached.

Remember that "mitre" applies to the width of the bevel, not the length. You will notice that the bevel looks rounded when it come off the roughing stone. The reason the

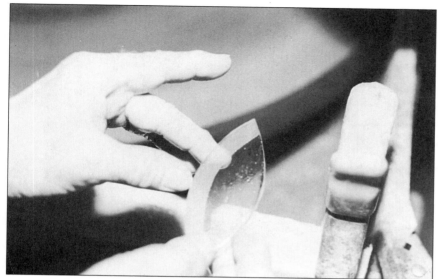

Holding the glass up for inspection. Note how straight the mitre is and that the outside curve flows nicely from top to bottom. Courtesy of Star Bevel.

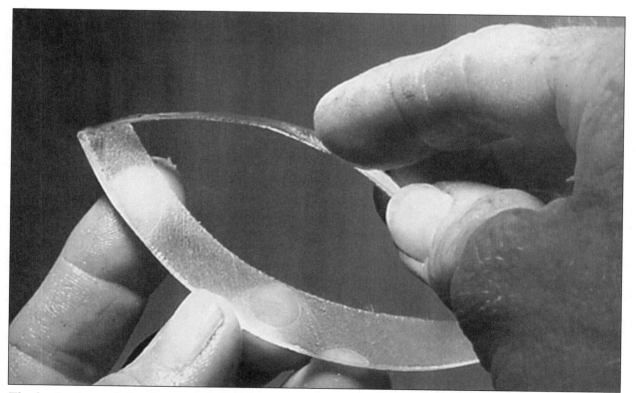

The beginnings of the shape of the bevel. This shows the results from the first station - the cast-iron wheel. The angle of the mitre is determined here and at this stage, the bevel has "sand" texture. Courtesy of Star Bevel.

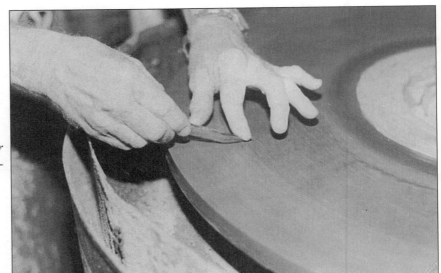

Back to the wheel to do the other outside curve of the glass. Courtesy of Star Bevel.

Finishing beveling the second outside curve. Courtesy of Star Bevel.

After the initial shaping is done on the cast-iron wheel, the bevel moves to the smoothing wheel. This shows the amount of slurry that accumulates on the glass as it is being worked on the wheel. Constant rinsing in the water dip bucket is necessary to see what is taking shape under your fingers. The bevel is moved on the wheel on a diagonal direction opposite the sand marks made by the cast-iron wheel to wear away the sand. Courtesy of Star Bevel.

The bevel with the top half smoothed and the bottom still showing sand for comparison.

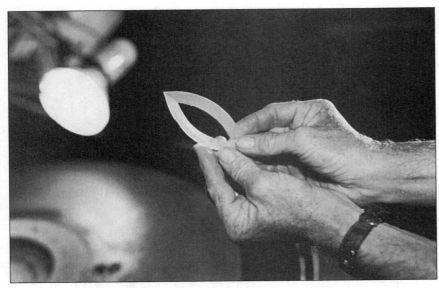

The roughed bevel opaqued along its mitres from the grinding action of the roughing wheel.

bevel is rounded is that the abrasive on the wheel doesn't allow the glass to contact the surface of the wheel in a flat manner. But this will be made up on the smoothing stone where the glass contacts the surface directly with just water between wheel and glass. The rounded mitre flattens right out.

Beveling a Circle

When you work with a circle, try to relate glass edge to beveled edge since there are no sides. There is no way you can do a circular bevel in one swoop. You must do it a section at a time, roughing it out slowly and trying not to allow flat spots or facets to intrude between these work areas. The rhythm is important in beveling a circle. It is important to know when to leave an area and move onto the next. It is also important that you have a fairly large piece of glass to bevel. The smaller the glass, the more difficult it is to hold against the wheel. A reasonable beveled circle might be 4" in diameter. Circles get smaller more rapidly than you might think,

as you try constantly to even up the bevel. Pretty soon you are beveling your fingers.

Away From the Wheel Vs. Against the Wheel

As you stand facing the cast-iron wheel, you will notice that it (probably) turns clockwise. This means that you can use it in two ways: you can hold your glass to the right hand side of the wheel, in which case the wheel surface will be passing toward you, pushing at the glass. Or you can hold the glass to the left hand side of the wheel, in which case the pull will be away from you. Some workers prefer one side of the wheel, others the other side. So far as the grinding effect is concerned, there is really little difference. There is a difference in the degree of comfort in holding the glass. You may be able to achieve more pressure of glass to wheel with the force of the wheel driving at you rather than away from you. This is particularly true when grinding circles and outside curves. On the other hand you may find that you can guide the glass best with the wheel spinning away from you. There appears to be a difference in choice only when small pieces are being ground, or at least pieces that do not take up the major surface of the wheel.

Inside Curves

It is certainly possible to do inside curves on the horizontal cast-iron wheel, but it is much simpler to do them on a vertical wheel. This technique is limited, however, because you must use the edge of the wheel and work in a downward direction from it. On the horizontal wheel you are limited as to size since the boxing of the machine doesn't allow for over-size pieces. On a single station cast-iron wheel you can do inside curves on very large pieces since no other stations (as in the combined beveling machine) are in the way. On standard machines you will use the outside edge of the wheel anywhere from 1/4" to 1/8", depending on how tight your curve is. I find it best to work against the spin of the wheel here. You can hold the glass firmly and guide the curve slowly along the entire edge. A vertical wheel of this nature is usually a diamond wheel, which cuts very fast and your initial project here may disappear before your eyes as the glass is abraded practically at the speed of light. So be careful and modulate your pressure. You can't use a cast-iron vertical wheel because the slurry would fly right off the rim before you could ever get your glass in place.

When doing inside curves on a horizontal wheel, use some extra water in the slurry to make sure the slurry will reach out to the rim. Since the cast-iron wheel is perfectly flat, you don't have to worry about any pitch of the wheel throwing off your curve.

Using A Diamond (Vertical) Wheel

The first thing you want to do with your diamond wheel is turn the water onto it. You must keep the diamond wheel wet; running it dry against the glass will ruin the wheel. Keep a wet sponge below it, touching the surface of the wheel. This is not to keep the wheel wet (the water jet will do that), but to keep the water from splashing you. The diamond wheel I recommend

The Denver Glass Machinery vertical beveler surrounded by items to keep the spray down and others to keep the wheels wet. This tabletop model allows for the use of two beveling wheels, one of which is often a diamond wheel. Courtesy of Star Bevel.

The spray from the water used to wet the vertical wheel must be carefully calculated if you don't want to get a bath. One way to maintain a steady and accurate flow of water onto the wheel is with a flex hose like the one shown. The hose is joined so it can be bent and angled in any position. Courtesy of Star Bevel.

is 100 grit, so if you are using 100 grit silicon carbide on the cast-iron wheel, you will get the same effect with the diamond. Actually you will probably find that the diamond wheel is quicker and cleaner than the cast-iron one. It is, of course, rotating more swiftly than the horizontal wheel because it is smaller. Other than that, it does cut better. You will find you have to use a firmer pressure with the diamond wheel than with the cast-iron wheel.

Even before you touch the glass to the wheel you will see another considerable difference between this wheel and the cast-iron one: the diamond wheel splashes water at you. Wear an apron and expect to get wet. This, of course, adds to the excitement of making your first bevel with the diamond wheel.

Vertical wheels can also be positioned on a long shaft turned by a motor. Various wheels can then be applied. Here the worker is beveling on a diamond wheel, using the edge of the wheel to produce an inside curve. Courtesy of Star Bevel.

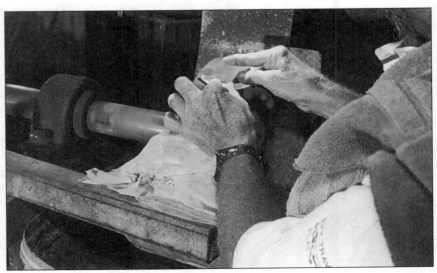

The pressure of the glass against the wheel is even more critical with the diamond wheel than with the cast-iron one. As mentioned, for one thing, the diamond wheel turns more rapidly than the cast-iron one so the pressure is thereby magnified. Too soft a pressure over a long period of time can ruin a diamond wheel and too strong a pressure can cause you to lose control of the piece and scallop the bevel. So don't be in a hurry to get the job done quickly. Actually, there is something about using the diamond wheel that makes one feel all too powerful and in control. Just remember: you are supposed to be doing the grinding, not the wheel.

The Second Station: Smoothing

The smoothing stone is the fairy god-mother of the beveling process, turning the ground glass edge of the piece into an actual (though far from complete) bevel. Whether the bevel in question will be a good or a bad one is also a function of the smoothing wheel. Every step beyond this second one will only add luster to what the smoothing stone has accomplished, either for good or for bad. The polishing wheels to come will shine up facets as well as smooth bevels. Very little glass will be removed once the smoothing stone has done its work.

I use an aluminum oxide stone wheel for my smoothing wheel, which must have water running on it at all times while it is in use. The wheel is the abrasive, the water the coolant. A new aluminum oxide stone wheel will at first absorb water into the wheel directly under the spigot. The water will, therefore, not directly flow out over the surface of the wheel. After a short time, however, the stone will begin to hold water on the surface, allowing for spark-free smoothing.

Without the water, the friction from glass to stone will heat up and can throw sparks.

Use your supply of paper towels to wipe the glass so that you can see how the smoothing is progressing. To see what you have accomplished you must actually pick up the glass, dry it, and look at it with direct natural reflected light. If you see sand, you must get rid of it with this wheel.

There is another difference between this wheel, or stone, and the roughing wheel. The roughing wheel, as I have noted, is flat; this is not true of the smoothing wheel. When the manufacturer dresses this wheel he puts a four degree pitch on it. The purpose of the pitch is to cut down the amount of drag this stone produces. If this wheel were perfectly flat, the entire bevel would rest on the surface at one time. This would make the drag so great that it would be all but impossible to hold onto the glass. Also, this pitch allows you to get your fingers under the glass which wouldn't be possible if the stone were flat.

But, you may say, the cast-iron wheel is perfectly flat and the drag is not all that great. True, but with the cast-iron wheel you have the grit between the bevel and the wheel surface. This breaks the drag. On the smoothing stone you are grinding directly on the surface. That can make for a lot of drag.

The aluminum oxide stone is not really a natural stone at all. It is manmade. However, the terms stone and wheel are used interchangeably and I refer to the item both ways. The point is, the aluminum oxide stone can be cast from a mold with a pitch already imposed. If it is not imposed, it is put on with a special machine. The thing to remember is that the pitch is there.

Smoothing Stone Technique

On the smoothing stone there is no traveling back and forth with the glass as with the

The smoothing stone in action. Note how firmly the worker is holding onto the glass against the drag of the stone.

cast-iron wheel. You will notice, as you place your bevel upon the stone, that a bubble appears at the point of contact. The bubble indicates where the cutting or wearing surface is located; in other words, where the action is occurring. It is in this spot that glass is being removed. The technique of smoothing is directly related to this bubble. The bubble is at once the indicator, the guide, and the critic of your performance. The idea is to move that cutting surface, the bubble, equally back and forth across the bevel. The more evenly you move it, the fewer facets you will end up with. To get the bubble to move and to flow evenly under the bevel area you must tilt the glass, raise its edges. Facets are caused by the bubble pausing in its shuttle back and forth to a greater or lesser extent. A very short pause, a slight tilting of the glass even for a split second out of rhythm is enough to cause a facet.

What you must learn to do is to pull down on the bevel until you see the bubble going from edge to edge and then start rocking the glass back and forth at that time. The bubble will all but disappear when it comes to the edge of the mitre but will reappear as you

begin to rock the glass back. Watch your pressure and try to keep it as constant as you can. Remember this wheel has a tremendous amount of drag so use less pressure than you did on the roughing wheel until you get used to the feel of this one. When you first start with the smoothing stone it is a good idea to practice on some waste bevels until you get a "hand sense" of the character of this wheel. After you have become more or less accustomed to the drag, it can be a bit of a shock. Some beginners actually have their glass snatched from their hands by this drag. So go ahead and apply your rough pieces. Use a moderate pressure to remove the sand. Then, to remove any facets that you might have caused, do a "feather" smoothing, obviously a very light fast smoothing and since it is or will become one of the major factors in your technique with this stone, it is a good idea to get into practice with it at the beginning.

As you start to smooth don't concentrate on any particular sandy areas; just keep working over the entire surface of the bevel. This will get you to these areas as a part of the whole. Again, this advice is to prevent

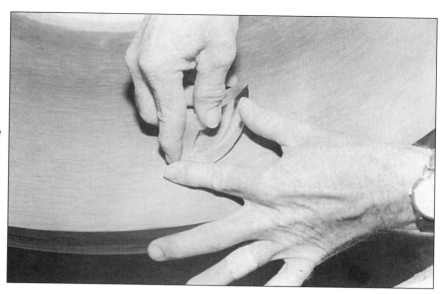

Tipping the glass back and forth on the smoothing stone. Courtesy of Star Bevel.

you from causing facets by concentrating too much on a particular region of the bevel. As you go along smoothing your surface, you will see that it begins to flatten any slight belly or uneven surface you may have brought from the cast-iron stone.

If you have a ridge or any other uneven surface, you will notice that when the bubble gets to that place, it will deform. It can split or elongate or twist. As you work your surface on the stone, the surface of the glass will become flat and your bubble will become bigger and wider. If the bubble deforms it means it is not fully contacting the glass and the stone at that high point. The bubble is quick to tell you what your glass surface is like.

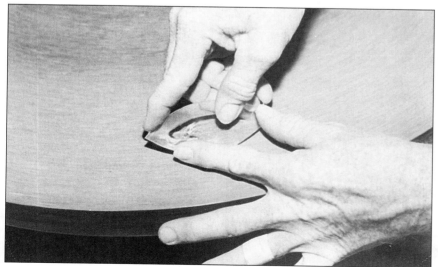

Watching the bubble just above the index finger. Courtesy of Star Bevel.

Completing the smoothing of the bevel working near the edge of the wheel on the right side. From this side, the glass is pushed onto the surface of the stone. Courtesy of Star Bevel.

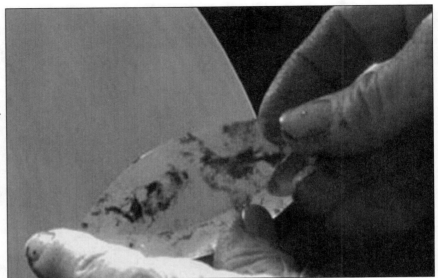

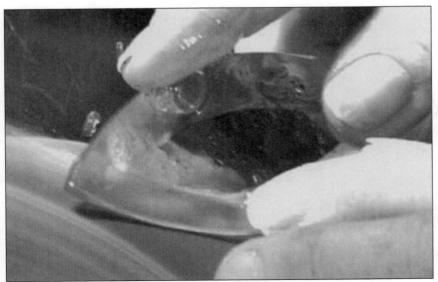

Close-up of the bevel being held on the smoothing wheel. Note the position of the glass in relation to the flat surface of the stone and water spray flying off the underside of the bevel. Courtesy of Star Bevel.

Keeping Your Stone Lubricated

The only lubricant or coolant used on the smoothing stone is water. This rule applies to both natural sandstone and aluminum oxide stones. The amount of water you have flowing on the wheel will depend on how fast you want to remove the glass as opposed to how much you want to ease the drag or pull of the wheel on your glass. In other words, a smaller amount of water dripping on your wheel will speed cutting but increase drag. The opposite is also true: a greater amount of water will make it much simpler to hold the glass against the stone, but the smoothing process will take a lot longer as the glass is really riding on a cushion of water rather than bearing directly against the grinding surface of the stone.

In time you will find a happy medium between the cutting speed and the amount of drag you want to put up with. If your stone surface is not sufficiently wet, or, as can happen, you start to use it forgetting to turn on the water at all, you'll quickly be reminded by the sparks that will appear between your stone and glass. These are quick flashes, not quite sparks, that will do no harm to stone or glass if the process is not extended unduly. There is, of course, no reason it should be. What it does is remind you that the stone surface is not wet. Don't be embarrassed if this happens to you; we have all had this particular memory lapse.

Cleaning the Sandstone

Cleaning stones involves removing various contaminants from the surface, particularly glass particles. The sandstone wheel tends to glaze after a time from the grinding process. To a certain extent this glazing can be helpful.

Once the wheel forms a glaze it cuts or grinds more smoothly than before. It doesn't grind quite as fast as before, but you might want to overlook the additional time spent for the soft quality of the smooth surface. The smoothing wheel works well when it has a certain amount of glaze on it; however, if too much glaze builds up, the grinding will really slow down. What you have to do then is break the glaze. The easiest way to do this is to pass a piece of emery cloth over the surface of the wheel while it is running dry. This will effectively remove all the glaze or, if you are careful, leave just enough to continue to provide that nice satin finish to the glass. Emery cloth is so fine that you can't apply too much pressure and actually change the shape of the wheel in any way. You can easily tell when the glaze is removed by the loss of the shiny surface and the more rapid grinding.

In using emery cloth to clean the stone, you can hold it to the stone by hand, although some uncomfortable friction may develop, or you can wrap it around a block of wood. The length of time you hold the emery cloth to the wheel depends on how much the wheel needs to be cleaned. If bits of grit from the cast-iron wheel have become partly imbedded, you might be able to remove them by hand with a swipe of the emery cloth. In other instances, you might have to hold the emery cloth wrapped in a block of wood to the wheel for 15 minutes or so. I favor 120 grit or even slightly finer emery cloth for this purpose.

The Third Station: Semi-polishing

Once you are done with the smoothing wheel, you are ready to semi-polish with either of the two wheels used for that purpose. The cork wheel and the fiber wheel are the two usually used, but other material has also been employed by various manufacturers of beveling machines. For my purpose here I will stay with the cork and the fiber wheels. In addition to removing the haze from the bevel as it comes from the smoothing wheel, semi-polishing removes any defects that have occurred in the previous two stations. However, you might get quite a high polish from the cork wheel. Many of the old time bevelers did just this. In fact, they got such a high polish that they stopped at the cork station, thus saving time and money. You don't want to do this and that's why I make the distinction between semi-polishing and high polishing. Each step in the beveling process contributes to the final product and to attempt to combine any two stages into one invariably diminishes the final product in some way.

The cork wheel is a vertical wheel and is made of real cork which has been found to be the best material for the purpose. Leather has been tried as a substitute but it has been found wanting. The cork on the wheel will last indefinitely unless you cut into it with your glass.

The cork wheel is not used alone. Pumice is applied to its surface and this can create a problem because the stuff tends to fly all over. Be prepared. The cork wheel can straighten out a number of problems, such as getting rid of minor scratches and removing deep haze and even removing some final specks of sand. But the wheel can cause some problems as well. You can blur your mitres by running over the break lines of the bevels and you can get pumice lines.

Pumice is a powder; to use it with the cork wheel you add water to make it into a paste. I use a half and half mixture. There are various grits of pumice, from fine to coarse. I use the extra coarse variety when I use a cork wheel.

Generally I prefer using a fiber wheel to the cork wheel. The fiber wheel was devised as a substitute for the cork wheel and its main advantage is that it has 600 grit silicon carbide imbedded in its mylar fiber so no other compound is necessary and it won't throw a surface compound at you. However, it does take a lot of water so it does tend to splash the water at you, which puts it right in there with its cousins the cork and felt wheels (the felt wheel is the final wheel which I will discuss in a moment).

A fiber wheel to polish the edge of the glass. This one has been modified by cutting a groove into the rim so both sides of the bevel can be polished at one time.

This is a vertical wheel, the one shown is an exceptionally large one and fairly expensive, but you can't beat it for giving that final polish. Courtesy of Star Bevel.

Before using the fiber wheel, soak it thoroughly in water. Once it is soaked there is no reason to put a sponge under it to cut down on its water-splashing habit since this wheel will only tear up the sponge and throw the pieces at you. It may also be more apt to bite your fingers than any other wheel, so be warned.

As the fiber wheel dries out it turns a light brown; you must add more water at this point. The fiber wheel will soften the mitres of your bevels much more rapidly than the cork wheel so you must be especially careful of these angles. Alas, you also will have no bubble here to use as a guide. All your work must be done by feel and experience.

The fiber wheel is great for removing facets and for applying a nice shine to your bevels, though not the shine the next wheel, the felt wheel, will provide.

The Fourth Station: High Polishing with the Felt Wheel

This is the final stage of the beveling progression. The felt wheel, the last of the wheels, like the cork wheel, is not used alone. It is also a vertical wheel. Either jeweler's rouge or cerium oxide is used with the felt wheel. I prefer cerium oxide, which I apply with a scrub brush. The bristles of the scrub brush lift up the nap of the felt and work the cerium oxide directly into the surface. Even so, the cerium oxide flies about even worse than pumice.

A difference from the cork wheel which uses no water, the felt wheel uses water but only to a degree. Felt is a water-absorbent material so there is a difference between when the wheel is turning and when it is standing still. Water must therefore be used judiciously. If you run the felt wheel too dry,

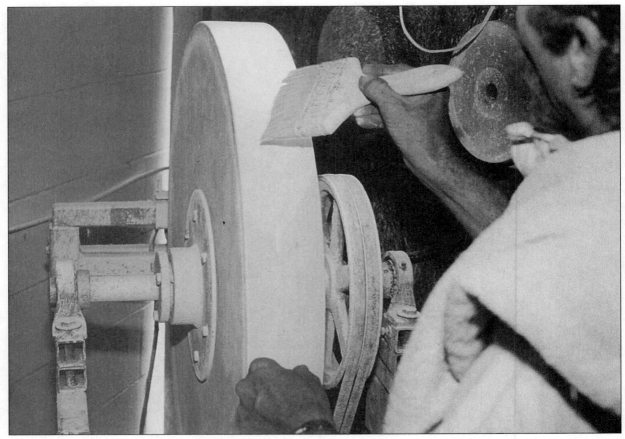

Loading the cerium oxide into the nap of the felt wheel. You can use a stiff paintbrush or a scrub brush to get the material placed properly. Courtesy of Star Bevel.

it will heat the glass from friction and possibly crack it. It's acceptable to have water running on the wheel while it is turning, but once it gets wet and you turn off the machine, all the water in the wheel tends to seep to the bottom. This is a problem because it leaves the surface of the wheel unevenly wet. I avoid this problem by mixing the cerium oxide very wet and putting it on a dry wheel with the scrub brush. I use no water from the spigot unless I have a lot of polishing to do and intend to keep the wheel running. You

will have to achieve this sort of water balance in the wheel as you go along.

On the felt wheel the glass bevel will become hot from friction in order to remove whatever pumice lines have come over from the cork wheel, if that's what you used. So long as this is "wet-hot" heat rather than "dry-hot" heat, the purpose will be served. Dry-hot heat, where the wheel doesn't have enough water, will usually crack the glass. You want this proper friction heat to "flow" the glass you are polishing.

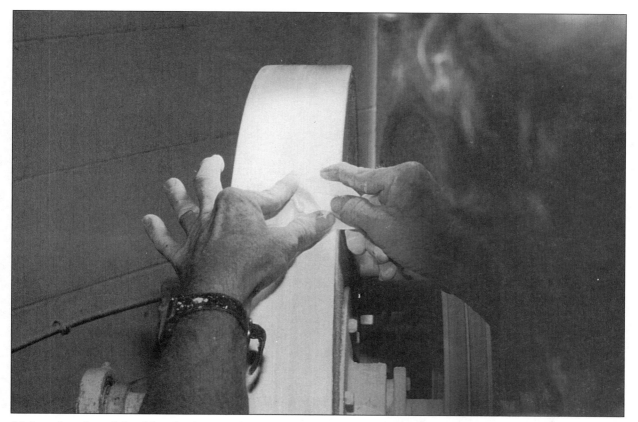

Using the edge of the felt wheel to produce a high polish on a small bevel. This size felt wheel will polish very large bevels with ease. Courtesy of Star Bevel.

Try to do a continuous polishing rather than a stopping and starting and holding the glass up to see what a fine job you are doing. Such an erratic rhythm will never build up the proper friction heat to do the job properly. Also, the more pressure you apply, the faster you can polish, but remember to hold your glass firmly. The felt wheel is a great glass grabber.

Combining Beveling and Engraving

Some old-time vertical wheel beveling machines allow placement for an engraving wheel on the common shaft. This is a convenient coalition and shows how closely related the two techniques really are. In my studio, I have a separate beveling and engraving machine in different parts of the room. I suspect, however, when I turn off the lights at night, they somehow get together and discuss their common interests.

Chapter Nine:
Project: A Flower Ensemble

This is a flower ensemble with several stalks of wheat courtesy of Kim Kostuch of Studio One, Milwaukee. Wheat is a favorite motif for the engraver; it happens to be easy to do though it looks quite difficult, and it gives a dramatic effect. (By the way, don't give away all secrets to anyone who admires your work. The fact that engraving is not as

The finished flower ensemble engraving.

This design can be enlarged or reduced to fit the piece of glass you've chosen and traced onto the glass surface with waterproof marker or india ink.

difficult as it appears is a fact most engravers keep to themselves.)

The flower ensemble design can be engraved with three wheels and some dremel (or hand piece) cutting. Use the olive wheel for the petals, the printy wheel for the circular centers, and the mitre wheel for the stems and veins.

Size

The size of the finished piece is a primary consideration. You don't want to lose the delicacy of the work, yet you do want the various elements large enough to show up. A good size for the average square design is 5" x 5". A good oval size is 6" x 4". These sizes fit nicely in people's windows and are just about right for bookends or paperweights or any of the multiple uses to which people put engraved glass pieces.

Bevel or No Bevel?

It certainly isn't mandatory to work with a beveled piece of glass, though the beveled edges add luster to the engraving by forming a sheen of light around it. Your design, however, should be calculated as to whether or not a beveled edge will be used. Obviously you don't want a design that will go right to the glass edge if a bevel is planned to take up that space. And, if no bevel is to be present, you may want to use that space either positively or negatively to accommodate part of your design.

In the finished piece shown, there is a bevel, since the flower ensemble design works quite well with one. The beveling process is covered in Chapter Eight.

Calculating Key Points

In taking the design from paper to glass, be careful how you position it on the glass blank. Think ahead to those key areas where you will start your first cuts. Usually these are the easiest areas to get into. Once you get these key cuts in place, they form a sort of skeletal structure for the rest of the engraving, and the rest of the cuts will fall in place. In other words, you don't have to cut every line with your first wheel and then re-cut everything with your second wheel.

If you are an advanced worker making more than one finished product, you might not have to draw the complete design on each glass blank. You can draw it on the first one and then just mark some key points on the other blanks. As a beginner, you should draw the design fully on each blank. Since this is hand work, not machine work, none of the blanks will be precisely the same no matter how carefully you try to make them so.

Step by Step

Different designs require different wheels, but I start with the olive wheel because I always start with the flower portion of a flower design, and that calls for the olive wheel. I find it is always easier to run the lines (stems) to the flowers than it is to pop the flowers onto the ends of these lines.

For this project you might just use a magic marker and rub the ink away as you are done with each area. Ink that doesn't come off can get in the way.

You have to be very, very careful to space the flowers properly. Keep in mind you will have to run stem lines to them.

I always see the design better with the spot lamp rather than with fluorescent light. I point the spot lamp at the wheel. With the light and dark points right at my working spot, I can see exactly where I am cutting. Precision is essential in engraving.

As you watch the carving in progress, you will see the water whipping around the area being carved, creating a sort of bubble. This effect tends to make the carved area look larger than it is. You have to train your eye to look through that water and see where the actual cutting is taking place. Don't be fooled by the bubble. The bubble tells you where you are, but not where the cutting is taking place; it doesn't provide a discrete enough area and will fool you when you try to make the same size perfect cuts in a row. Admittedly, this kind of calculating is a formidable task for a beginner; however, it's something that will come to you as you progress. The main thing to understand is that if you go by the bubble to calculate size, you will be way off. This is always a source of frustration to even trained workers and, despite my warning, you will probably fall into this trap. If you remember to use the bubble as an indicator of, rather than the size of the site of the cutting, you will be able to work with it instead of having it work against you.

Carving the Petals

Prepare to exercise patience when carving the petals, since all of them have to be even, which doesn't necessarily mean identical. Some beginners try to match up the petals perfectly, adding increments to each, making them larger and larger until they run out of room on the glass blank. Follow your inked design, but don't be concerned if each petal isn't exactly like the last one. You will have enough to think about just getting the petals even without worrying about matching them perfectly.

One problem with doing petals (or any such portion of a design) can be over-concentrating. Avoid concentrating too much on one petal or that spot will tend to take over. While attending to the specific area you are working on, keep looking at the overall - the whole design. When shaping a flower, remember the basic flower shape even while concentrating on its elements. Concentrate on the object as a whole rather than on individual cuts. Being able to do this - to keep an eye on the overall rather than the individual elements - will prevent a flower that's tilted or deformed

When I work on more than one blank at a time, I skip from one to the other, like a bee from flower to flower, and then come back to the first one. I wipe out all my ink lines as soon as I'm finished with them. Of course, if you are using india ink/shellac, you can't wipe off the marks. The first few times you engrave, you will probably feel more secure putting your design on with india ink; after you've done a few, try engraving and wiping out the marks as you go. This provides a feeling of looseness, less constraint, and more artistic control. Don't let this freedom lead you beyond the design limits, however.

Adding the Stems

Once the flower petals are in, move on to the stems. Change to a mitre wheel to cut in the finer stems. The heavier stems and the ribbon bow at the bottom are done with the strap wheel. If you do the stem lines awkwardly, you can ruin the whole piece, so take care. The stem lines are linear guides for the eye so don't put them in any old way. I find it easier to start the lines by first carving the center line and working from the center to either side. Bisecting the space is a way of reading the space.

To do a flower with many, many points, use the mitre wheel to make all the deep cuts, each time bisecting an area. In this manner you get all the cuts point-to-point equally spaced. You couldn't do it as well starting with the first cut and moving consecutively round the circle.

The stem lines go in very, very fast. You probably won't need to mark where the petal lines go, though as a beginner you might want to. Actually you shouldn't need to; you should get enough of a feeling as to where the petals lines go to follow the design.

Adding Detail

Add detail to the flowers with the mitre wheel. Up to now, you may have been a little disappointed to see the process being a bit barren of detail. So here goes: add some detail in the leaves, enhancing the already nice design. Keep working over the design as laid down to provide detail and character. You may want to change mitre wheels to one that tapers very gradually. This will give a different aspect than the narrower mitre you have been using. I use this wide tapered mitre wheel to carve the wheat. This wheel is so good for wheat that I call it the wheat wheel.

After the wheat has been carved in, you've got all the basic elements. It still may not look like much, but as you add more detail the work begins to come alive. Don't expect your engraving to leap right out at you immediately. At first it may look simple and flat. But as it starts to go together it will develop a character of its own; hopefully the one you intended. As a final touch, use the dremel tool to add some freehand stippling. Make sure you have enough water to lubricate the dremel bit. You don't want to crack the glass at this point.

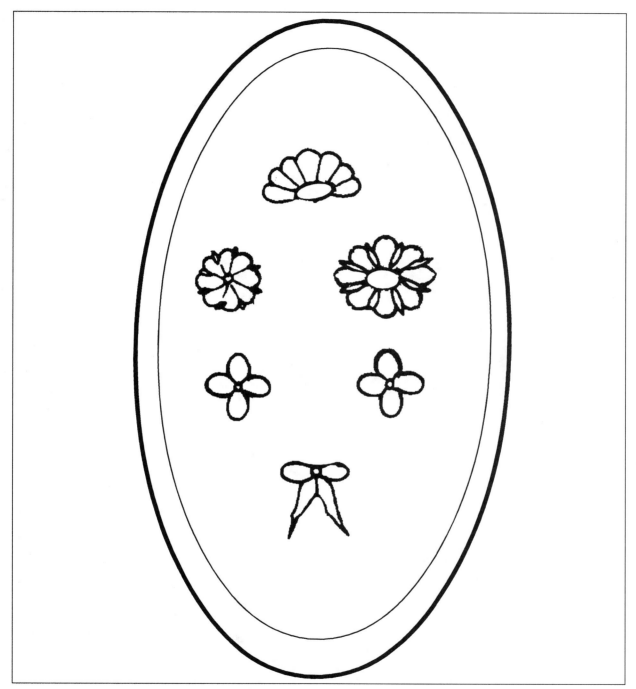

Start by carving the flowers with the olive wheel. It's important to visualize the spatial relationship of these items before beginning to engrave. To keep things simple, choose a balanced design. Remember to allow room for the stems.

Cut in the stems with a mitre wheel, running them up to the flower petals. This is easier than doing the stems first and adding the flowers at the end of each. Switch to a strap wheel to do the heavier stems and the ribbon bow at the bottom.

Carve the detail in the petals with the mitre wheel.

The wheat has been added using a special mitre wheel I call the wheat wheel, although any mitre wheel will do the job. I have one with a slightly wider mitre that makes doing wheat a cinch. Wheat is merely a collection of small cuts made by holding the glass momentarily to the wheel at the proper angle.

Chapter Ten: Special Effects

Eyeglass Engraving

An engraved design on an eyeglass lens can make a unique gift and the engraving is fun and easy to do. Use caution and restraint though - if you go too far, you're liable to ruin the glasses. Of course, you won't engrave the entire lens of an eyeglass, you'll just put a tiny design in the corner. To do this, you'll use a tiny, tiny wheel and produce a very nice little motif such as a flower or star in the corner of the lens. You can do engraving on plastic lenses too.

For this type of engraving, the engraving wheel must be really small and must spin

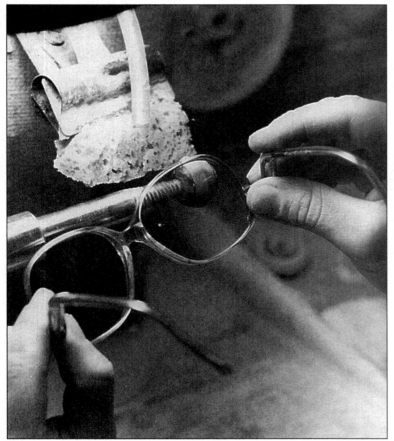

The mitre wheel used to engrave at this small scale is about the size of a cherry tomato. This type of engraving is very exact, so place the lens against the slowly turning wheel very carefully.

The finished star sparkles in the corner of one lens without interfering with the line of vision.

very slowly. This is about the slowest rpm I use in engraving, maybe 400 rpms or less. It depends on the design. The only other time I use the wheel as slowly is when I tap the wheel to get rid of wobble. It's important to use a slow rpm when engraving on eyeglasses because it allows for excellent control and if you do make a mistake, it will be a little one. If the wheel is spinning rapidly, one mistake can ruin the pair of glasses.

When engraving eyeglasses, you must maintain control of the design. Even with the best of intentions, you can make the design larger than you anticipated. The eye, however, doesn't get larger to compensate for a large design. When the glasses are off the face, the correct size design tends to look too small, almost lost on the lens, and the temptation to make it just a wee bit bigger is very strong. Don't give in to this temptation. You certainly don't want the design in the line of vision. The best way to keep your ambition in hand is to circle in ink the outer limits permissible to the engraving and not go beyond this circle no matter what your artistic impulse of the moment might be.

Before you begin this pretty exacting form of engraving (you don't want to ruin your own or someone else's eyeglasses), make sure the lenses are clean and carefully calculate and mark the area to be engraved.

Brilliant Work (Polishing)

In engraving, the term brilliant work refers to geometric patterns that have been cut very deep and polished to perfection.

Polishing is a totally separate operation from those so far discussed, and can be tedious, if rewarding to an extent. Polishing your pieces will double the time it takes to produce them, however, and unless you have cut very deep, you may not see much difference after all the work is done.

Ordinarily I don't polish my engraved pieces. I find it isn't necessary and rarely does the engraving go so deep or become so complex that facets are formed that would better reflect light from a polished surface. And it's extra work and messy work at that. However, there is nothing to keep you from polishing your work if you so desire.

To do so, you will need polishing wheels to correspond to your stone wheels in size and shape so they fit into the channels your stone wheels have cut. The polishing wheels themselves are merely carriers of the chemicals that do the work of polishing, namely pumice, for the first stage of polishing, and cerium oxide or jeweler's rouge for the final stage. Wheels used for polishing can be attached to the left hand shaft of the engraving machine. They are either cork or felt wheels.

Polishing, despite being time-consuming and messy, can be used not only to set work off to advantage (often covering flaws with a sheen of light), but as part of the artistic statement. For instance, in a floral piece you could polish the flowers and leave everything else a matte (natural) finish. Here is a totally different emphasis and effect from having everything the same. The result is a completely different statement.

Since polishing is so boring a task (to me, though some people love doing it), most studios that use the procedure generally have someone just learning thus employed. It's almost impossible to wreck a piece by polishing it, although you do have to exercise some care with the pumice by not pressing too hard. This can leave scratches if you become careless. But generally, in polishing you remove such a tiny amount of material it's safe to leave it to a helper.

Engraving Flashed Glass

Flashed glass is colored glass that has had a second color "flashed" over the first. The primary color can be yellow, green, white or what have you, so when you engrave away the top color, whatever color lies below shows through. This show-through color should be chosen to complement the engraved design. Flashed glass is available in a variety of sizes and colors from stained glass suppliers.

Engraving on flashed glass is an almost magical technique. The design appears so rapidly and with such verve that the effect is hard to resist; one almost wants to applaud. And why not? It's a great show.

The basic problem with engraving flashed glass is that you must choose a colored glass that is not so dark that you can't see through it to follow your inked-on pattern. In the ini-

Engraving on flashed glass is dramatic and quick. But don't be too quick. Flashed glass is very unforgiving and one wrong move will stand out accusingly since there is no way of putting the flashing back into the glass once it has been engraved away.

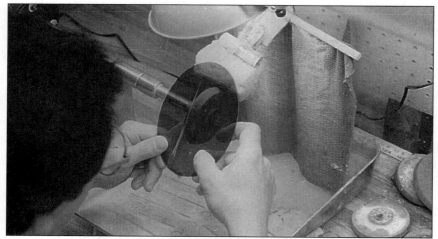

After cutting an oval from a piece of flashed glass and smoothing its edges with the strap wheel, use the mitre wheel to make the first two cuts, the beginning of a tree. Photos courtesy of Studio One.

To make the cuts for the tree branches, turn the glass.

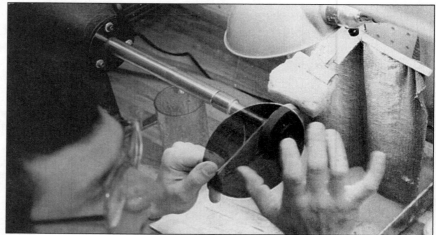

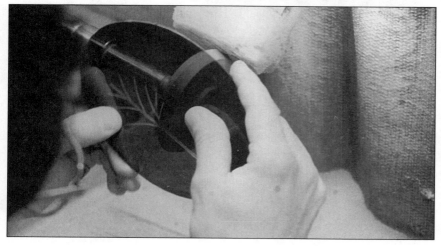

Turn the glass further to make the cuts for more branches.

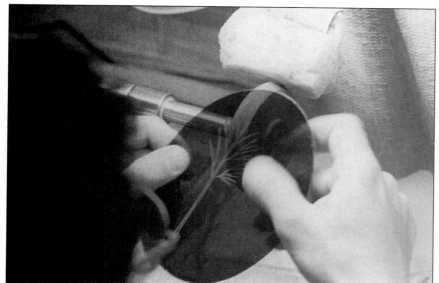

As the branches fork into smaller ones, make more delicate cuts.

Keep the glass continually in motion to get the best angle against the wheel as you add the branches. Note the way the trunk is formed, with the lines converging as they ascend.

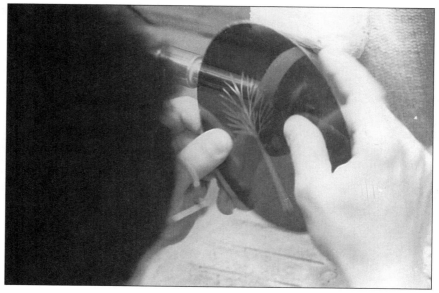

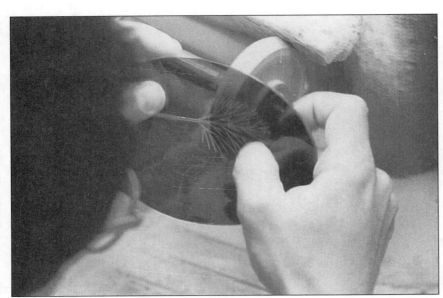

Turn the glass completely to one side to continue the branches.

After the tree is completed, make the beginning cuts to create the bird, still using the mitre wheel.

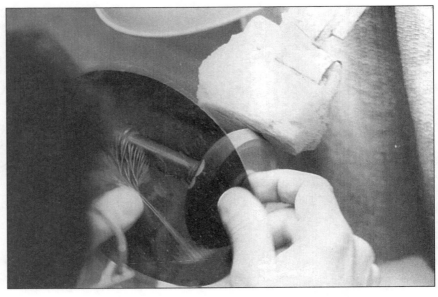

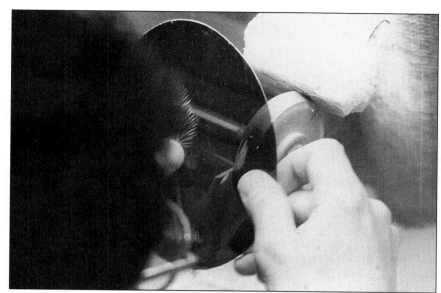

More cuts on the bird.

The final touches to the bird.

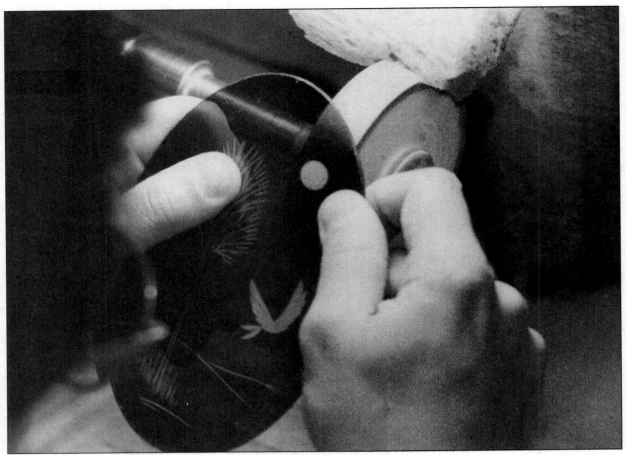

Change to a printy wheel to make the sun, which is just a circle.

tial enthusiasm of removing color, the temptation is to keep going and, indeed, this is fun for a while. But flashed glass is not a toy and, in the long run, the magic of working with it becomes, like any other glass, a matter of technique and forethought.

Drag Cutting: A Recapitulation

Because drag cutting is so essential to the engraving operation, I want to go through it once again, stressing pertinent points. For more information, refer to Chapter Five.

Drag cutting means working in a direction perpendicular to that of the wheel. Working the glass "with" the wheel means working it forward and backward, a "natural" direction. Dragging the glass across the wheel left to right means working harder and exercising more control of the glass than riding it up and down. Drag cutting may also be accomplished in a motion diagonal to that of the wheel; an even trickier sleight of hand.

Drag cutting is one of the most difficult engraving techniques; it takes the most practice to get right, and even after a lot of practicing, can still go wrong. It also creates many of the most spectacular effects of engraved glass.

Drag cutting provides different effects with different wheels. Dragging the olive wheel gives a mottled result or a roulade effect. But there are shapes you can achieve with all the wheels that really have no name and that are subject to the whims of the individual engraver. By combining shapes and combining wheels, you approach an elegant degree in this art form achievable by anyone willing to invest time to practice and learn. For example, consider a leaf, one of the more spectacular and (apparently) complex shapes. Yet a leaf can be formed merely by a diagonal drag going up the line of the stem (the mitre cut); while the stem is made thinner as it goes up by decreasing the pressure of the glass against the mitre wheel. The success of this technique lies in the hands - it is the motion of the hands that enlarges upon the shapes of the wheels. It may take a while for you to get there, but once you've mastered the motions, the hands and fingers never forget and the rest is merely a repetitive process.

The first time you try drag cutting, don't be humiliated if your glass skips, slips, or in other ways takes off on you. If you do manage to hang on, you may find the glass skidding over the wheel surface and making a mess. This is not abnormal for the first time, or even the second. Or the fifth. Don't berate yourself. Drag cutting invites your glass to skid. That's what drag cutting is: a controlled skid. Even at that, with an uncontrolled skid when you look at your piece of glass later you will find the "drag" full of interesting striations. You want more striations? Go back and re-drag the glass, adding more pressure and turning the angle slightly. And you can do it again. Each time you repeat the process, adding more pressure, turning the angle slightly, you will begin to find yourself making a leaf.

Learning to drag cut properly is one of the essentials of the engraving process. It makes the wheel do 90% of the detailed work for you. People will look at the finished product and assume you spent an hour putting in all those striations. The fact that the wheel did if for you in a matter of seconds is your little secret.

Chapter Eleven:
Patterns to Practice With

A Question of Practice

It's easy to tell a beginner to practice, but the question always comes back, practice with what? In this chapter you'll find a number of fairly basic designs you can use to improve your technique while having fun and producing practical results. Of course, you don't have to adhere strictly to these designs; you are encouraged to modify and enlarge upon them.

Patterns are courtesy of the author or Studio One Art Glass, Milwaukee, Wisconsin.

The butterfly panel offers specific challenges on its own, especially in the long leaves and the smaller design of the butterfly which calls for smaller wheels.

Diamond Beveled Panel

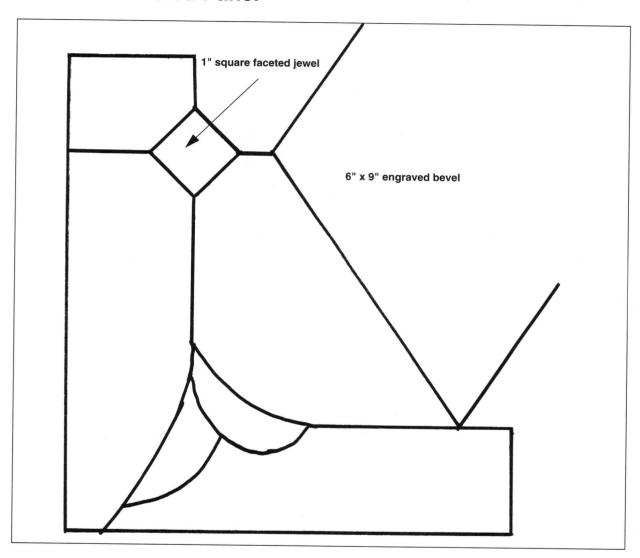

A portion of the diamond beveled panel. The bevel makes up the 6" x 9" center portion of the panel, enclosing whatever engraved design you choose. A 1" square faceted jewel is used to further set off the engraved centerpiece. Portions of the sides and bottom can be stained or clear glass. The stained glass pieces should be fairly large with a small number of cuts so as not to interfere with the central engraved bevel.

The repetitive design is as shown. Once again, the center can be a bevel with the engraved wildflower design, or regular glass. The design is calculated to go either way. Figure out which wheels you want to use, use each one to all its extent, then switch to the next. That's the most efficient way to work.

Hexagon Engraved Panel

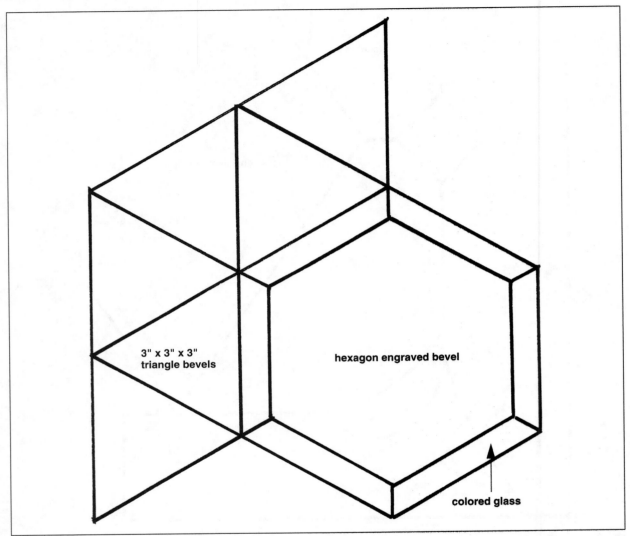

3" x 3" x 3"
triangle bevels

hexagon engraved bevel

colored glass

A variation on the diamond engraved bevel is a hexagonal one. Here the central hexagon engraved bevel is surrounded and emphasized by smaller triangle bevels not engraved. The central bevel is separated from the triangle bevels by a border of colored glass. This is a simple panel to put together inasmuch as the bevels that comprise 80% of it are all cut. All you need do is engrave the hexagon. You'll love the finished product!

Butterfly on a Mirror

This is a nice design for a mirror, a rectangular engraving measuring 6" by 9". Engraving a mirror utilizes the same techniques as engraving any other piece of glass. The effect is similar to sandblasting. This design takes up quite a bit of space, leaving only a small area to be used as a looking glass. This design can be modified to suit the size of the mirror. Note the way the design is balanced, with the motif very much present but not obtrusive. Engraving mirror is one way to combine craft and practicality. You can use other bevels around the mirror to further enhance the effect. Of course, this design can be used on plain glass as well.

The Bird and Tree Design

This design appears engraved on flashed glass on page 183. Before you begin engraving on flashed glass, make sure you're working on the side of the glass that is flashed. I've seen students make cuts deeper and deeper trying to find the change in color, until the glass breaks. It's not hard to tell which side is flashed - you can usually tell by looking at the edge of the glass. If you're still uncertain, scratch the surface with the point of a glass cutter. This design is a nice one to start with because it is instantly dramatic, easy to see the engraving figurations as they form, and is fun to do.

Trio of Flowers

A stained glass window with an engraved circular central bevel. The central design is offset by a circular stained glass break with interposed diamond jewels that emphasize the dramatic centerpiece. When doing such a work, be careful not to make the central engraving too busy. It's easy to get carried away when your enthusiasm takes over, so it's best to step back a few paces and observe the piece with a critical eye every now and then. This centerpiece is pretty full.

Single Rose

An engraved rose on an oval bevel. Strictly a decorative piece, this is a very popular design. It can be foiled and hung in a window or a hole can be drilled in the top for hanging.

Sample Patterns

Here's a selection of patterns to get you going in the right direction. Use them as is or make your own additions. Don't feel you have to copy them exactly. Enlarge or reduce them to fit the piece and add you own modifications. Good luck and have fun.

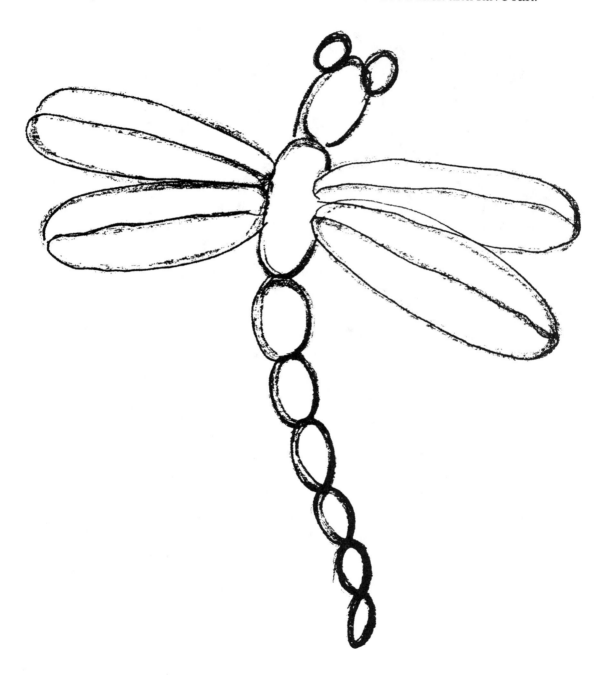

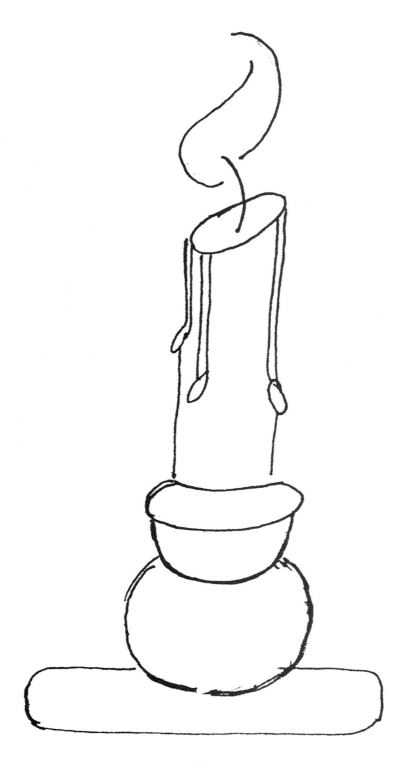

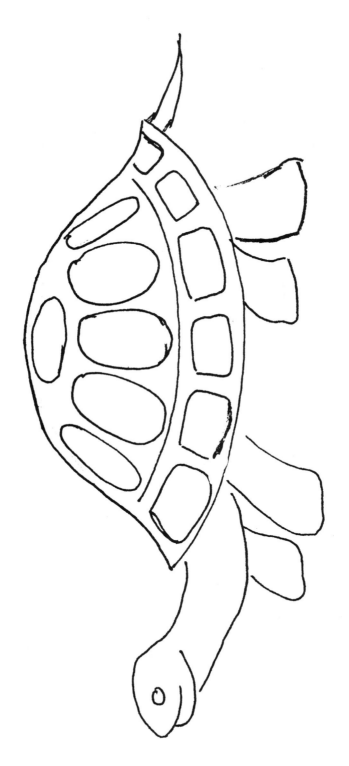

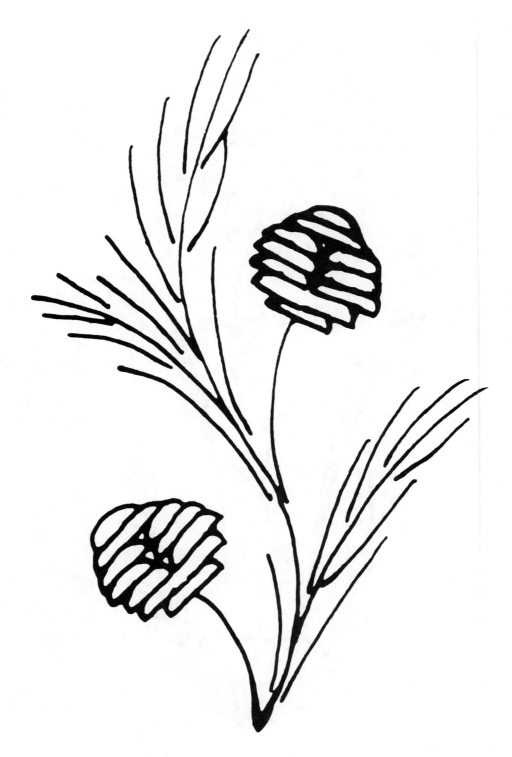

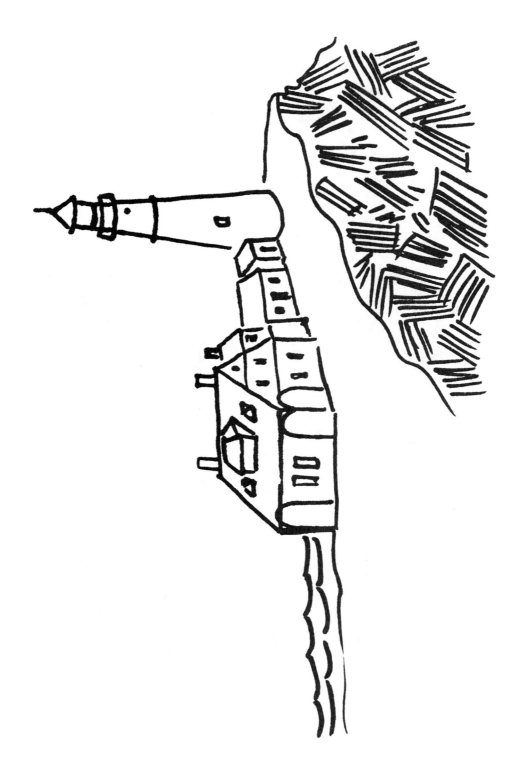

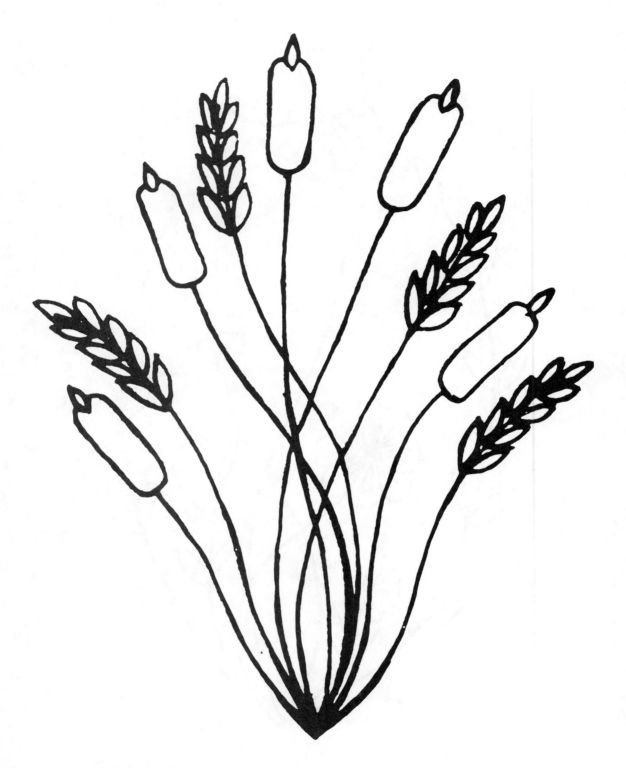

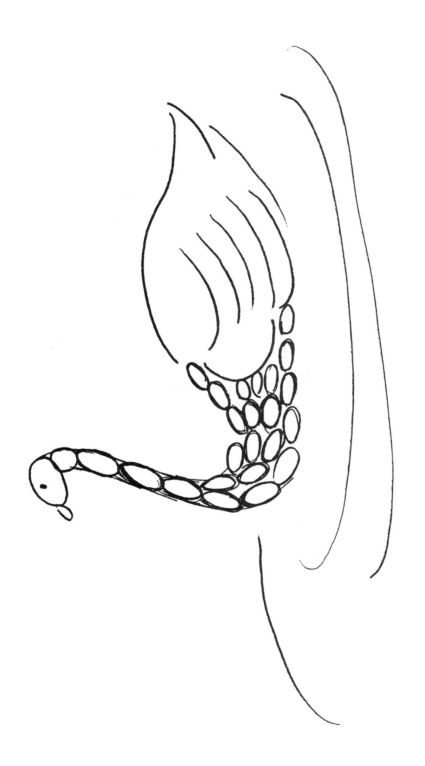

Index

shellac, 121
silicon carbide, 148
silicon carbide stick, 77, 78
siphon water system, 21
slat racks, 27, 28
slurry, 138, 154
smoothing wheel, 138, 163
soldering, 12
space, 26
speed, machine, 34
spindle, 12, 35
sponge, 22
stained glass, 12, 146
stance, 26
step bevel, 138
stone aluminum oxide wheel, 43
stone wheel engraving, 15
straight mandril, 36, 37, 38, 39, 40
strap wheel, 12, 44, 45, 48, 87

T

tapered mandril, 36, 39, 40
tapering, 138

tapping, 97
threaded mandril, 36
torch, 52, 53, 64
torque, 32, 33

V

vertical machine, 138

W

waste water, 21
water, 21
waves, 139
wheels, *see engraving wheels*
wobble, 50, 77
work area, 19
workbench, 25